I0149267

# PRAISE FOR *THE LETTERS OF JOHN: A PARTICIPATORY STUDY GUIDE*

The Letters of John are essential reading for today's Christian. They reveal a Christianity in the making, defining itself, charting its ethical course, and seeking to articulate a life-changing theological vision of Christ, embodied in the world and in our lives. In our pluralistic and polaristic time, in which many Christians fear cultural, religious, and political changes, we need to remember that faith flourishes when we choose love rather than fear. Bob Cornwall's text on the Letters of John invites us to engage first century Christianity in ways that will help us understand more clearly our vocation as Christians in our own time. The text is clear, articulate, and academically sound, ideal for congregational study groups and personal reflection. Bob Cornwall's interplay of theology, biblical studies, and spiritual practices will inspire and guide us in creative responses to our post-Christian, pluralistic and contentious time.

Bruce Epperly, PhD
Pastor and Author

Robert Cornwall has written a guide for a Bible study that is needed in churches today. There is solid background material for study that anyone, regardless of Bible study experience, can use well. The breakdown of material with reading scripture, a lesson, meditation and discussion questions, and a time for prayer is designed for wonderful deep conversations. This Bible study is needed today as it reminds us of who we are as the Body of Christ while inspiring us to love one another, live in truth, and work towards restoration.

Shauna Hyde, PhD
Pastor, Counselor, Author

Tucked away near the end of the 27 books that make up the Gospels and Letters, it is easy to forget the Letters of John or to think of them as sweet little notes on love. Through the eyes of theologian, minister, and biblical interpreter Robert Cornwall , we see these letters as muscular theological statements that John directed to electric theological controversies concerning the nature of Jesus and concerning the nature of relationships in the church and mission in community that are still taking place in congregations of all sizes and theological stripes today. Cornwall initially outlines the model of participatory Bible study that can structure each class session and that includes both placing the text in its historical context and meditating on the significance of text in disciplined ways while also identifying points of contact with church and world today. Along the way, he identifies—and respects—the different ways passages might be interpreted. Individual readers and study groups receive a double blessing: (1) a study focusing specifically on the Letters and (2) a model for studying other biblical texts. This book would be an ideal resource for studies and sermons—the congregation studies a passage during the week as background for the sermon on Sunday. The eleven chapters in the book would make an ideal structure for such an effort.

**Ronald J. Allen, PhD**
Professor of Preaching, and Gospels and Letters, Emeritus
Christian Theological Seminary


In this commentary, Bob Cornwall integrates well his scholarly abilities with pastoral concerns. In the letters of John we have a "theology on the ground," and Cornwall navigates us through the writer's theological concerns that relate to the ministry of John's community. This book is rich in its depth and practical in its application. Bob brings the message of the letters "that which was from the beginning," and speaks to the concerns of Christians in the twenty-first century.

**Allan R. Bevere, PhD**
Pastor, Ashland First United Methodist Church
and Professional Fellow in Theology,
Ashland Theological Seminary, Ashland, Ohio

# THE LETTERS OF JOHN

A Participatory Study Guide

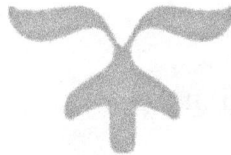

Robert D. Cornwall

Energion Publications
Gonzalez, Florida
2019

Copyright © 2019, Robert D. Cornwall

Unless otherwise marked, Scripture quotations are from New Revised Standard Version Bible, copyright © 1989 National Council of the Churches of Christ in the United States of America. Used by permission. All rights reserved worldwide.

Scriptures marked CEB are from the Common English Bible, copyright © 2012, Common English Bible.

Scripture quotations marked The Message are taken from THE MESSAGE, copyright © 1993, 2002, 2018 by Eugene H. Peterson. Used by permission of NavPress. All rights reserved. Represented by Tyndale House Publishers, Inc.Cover Design: Henry Neufeld
Stained Glass image: Adobe Stock, #64834710

ISBN13: 978-1-63199-688-7
LCCN: 2019940829


Energion Publications
PO Box 841
Gonzalez, FL 32560

https://energion.com
pubs@energion.com

# PREFACE

"What the world needs now is love, sweet love." Love is a central theme in the letters of John. The author of the first letter declares that "God is love." Indeed, we are to love one another, because *"love is from God"* (1 John 4:7). There is more to these letters than a message of love, or perhaps I might put it this way. While love stands at the heart of these letters, there are disturbing elements to these letters that might raise questions about the nature of the love proclaimed. In any case, these letters, which likely date to the end of the first and perhaps well into the second century give us a glimpse of how early Christians struggled to live faithfully in difficult times.

This study guide is intended to invite users (whether individuals or groups) to dive deep into the biblical story. You may find this journey into the text difficult at some points. You may also find it to be liberating at other points. The Bible cannot be read flatly, as if everything is equally giving voice to God's word. At the same time, when approached with care and reverence, I believe we can hear a word from God even in passages that shock and dismay us. We may decide to argue with the text, saying no to its implications. That is an appropriate way of engaging the text.

The series in which this study appears is intended to bring heart and head together. As the *Shema*, the Jewish confession of faith, invites adherents to *"love the Lord your God with all your heart, with all your soul, and with all your might,"* not only keeping the commandments, but also reciting them to one's children, talking *about them, binding them on your hands, fixing them on the foreheads, and writing them on the doorposts and gates* (Deuteronomy 6:4-9), so we will seek to love God with our entire being.

This book offers a study of the three Letters of John. It is part of the Participatory Bible Study series that was developed by Henry Neufeld, which seeks to build upon the devotional principles of the *lectio divina* model of reading scripture. It is an invitation to inhabit the text of Scripture, so that one might experience oneness with God. Although this has a strong devotional foundation to it, the method also invites critical investigation of the text.

The letters of John offer us an interesting opportunity to bring these two elements of biblical study together. There is much here that stirs the soul and draws one into the life of faith. There is theology and spiritual practice in these letters. These are pastoral messages that speak to congregations that may be experiencing spiritual challenges. In addition, it's possible that 1 John, which has few marks of a letter, could have been a sermon that was later shared with different congregations. There are also important critical questions to be answered as one explores these texts. Because we don't know the identity of the author(s) or the destination of these letters, it is difficult to read them contextually. We don't know the full back story to the words we read here. Many are attracted to the words about love, but they may also find the words about church discipline disturbing. My hope is that at the end of the study, participants and readers will not only have a better understanding of the text, but also find themselves moving toward a more mature faith in God. If we take the author of 1 John at his word, then the intention here is that what appears on the page was written "to you who believe in the name of the Son of God, so that you may know that you have eternal life" (1 John 5:13). It would appear that there is some uncertainty about such things as eternal life. Discernment of spirits is called for, for not all who claim to represent Christ are truly representatives of his mission. Thus, we have a word of hope and a word of warning.

Faith and understanding are not mutually exclusive categories, and this study seeks to draw them together. It is a study that can be undertaken by individuals in the quiet of their own homes, but it is also designed for use by groups. So, whether in groups or alone, my prayer is that you will experience the blessings of God's continuing grace.

Before the journey is undertaken, I must give thanks to Henry Neufeld, my publisher and editor for inviting me to participate in this series of studies. Henry laid the format of the study, which I have followed closely, but he also gave me the freedom to set my own tone and texture in writing this study. I'd like to also thank the members of my Wednesday Bible Study groups at Central Woodward Christian Church, who have been attentive to the study of scripture and have pushed themselves and me into new understandings of the faith. Finally, I wish to thank my wife Cheryl who has given me room to write works such as this, but most of all has been a constant companion in life.

# USING THIS BOOK

This study guide consists of two sections:[1]

1. Introductory information

2. Study sheets

As you prepare to enter this process of biblical study, it involves several steps reflecting the principles of *lectio divina*. You may have other ideas, or even a completely different method, and that is fine, but it will still help if you understand the starting point.

You should also have some kind of guideline for how you will approach your study. That guide is going to suggest a process of study, which I'll repeat briefly here:

1. Preparation, including materials, prayer, and opening your mind

2. Overview

3. Background

4. The inner cycle (or central loop): Meditate, Question, Research, Compare

---

1   Energion Publications offers a pamphlet with an outline of this study process and a list of resources. It is titled *I Want to Study the Bible*, and can be found on the site https://participatorystudyseries.com or on https://energiondirect.com. It is available in ebook formats as well as print.

5. Sharing

This is a study process and it says very little about what you might do at each step of the process. It is, however, built on the principles of *lectio divina*, or "holy reading." Let's summarize those principles first and then look at the steps and see how they will help you apply these same principles to your study.

## HOLY READING: A MODEL FOR BIBLE STUDY

Lectio divina, which means holy reading, is an ancient practice of studying scripture. There are many ways to practice lectio divina. It has been done in many ways since Origen described it around 220 CE. The great monastic traditions of the church further developed it into distinct phases and practices. The basic principle is that reading and studying the Bible should be remarkably different than reading the morning paper or studying Shakespeare. The Bible is a sacred text; it is a Living Word. It should not be, therefore, studied like as if it were a collection of dead pages from history.

When the two men were walking down the Road to Emmaus, they met the risen Christ, but did not recognize him (Luke 24). As they were walking down the road, Jesus interpreted to them the biblical story. Only later, as they were breaking bread, did they realize that Christ was with them the entire time.

Lectio Divina is a practice that, through the power of the Holy Spirit, invites the risen Christ to interpret scripture to us anew. It is a prayerful reading of scripture that expects God to speak once again through this Holy Word. Prayer should influence the way you study the Bible, and studying the Bible should influence the way you pray. In lectio divina, it is impossible to tell when you are studying and when you are praying, as there is no difference.

This practice is usually applied on small passages of scripture for an extended period of time. However, in this study lectio divina is used as a strategy to study an entire book of the Bible. This is somewhat challenging because the scripture text is so large, but the prayerful approach is still crucial to Christian study of the scripture. In these lessons, the ancient practice of lectio is blended with modern study methods that consider the historical, cultural, and literary contexts.

The historical methods are important to us because they help connect us to people of a different time and place who experienced the same God that we do, learned from the same texts, and were led by the same Spirit. In this context we do not study history for its own sake; we study history so that we might meet those who wrote the texts and those who have studied the passages before us.

The lessons in this guide are designed around the four movements of lectio divina established by Guigo II, a 12th century Carthusian monk, in a book called The Monk's Ladder. He organized the practice around four rungs that help us draw closer to God through reading the Bible.

**Reading (*lectio*):** The first rung of the ladder is reading. Believe it or not this is the step most often skipped or diminished. It is important to do the Bible reading for each lesson to get the most out of it. Ideally it should be read several times so that you can become familiar with the language and themes of the text. This book is a guide to help you study the biblical text. It is a supplement to the text itself, and the text of scripture should be the primary focus in your study. The steps of the participatory study method emphasize different ways of reading to help the text become part of you as you study.

**Meditating (*meditatio*):** The next step is to prayerfully meditate on the text. Dig deep into it. Study the words. Break it down into pieces. In this study this is where most of the background information is located. Look up words to find their meaning. Notice if there are any words or actions that the Holy Spirit may be leading you to examine further.

**Praying (*oratio*):** Third, we learn to pray the text. Use what you have learned from the scripture to formulate a prayer. It may be helpful to write it down. (There are note pages at the end of each chapter.) At the end of each lesson is a prayerful exercise that expounds on one of the themes from the text. Feel free to add your own prayers. This is where the text really becomes alive to us.

In the method used for this study guide, prayer is not seen as simply one part of the study; prayer permeates your study. You start with prayer and listening so that you will hear what God has to say through the text. Then you end by turning what you have heard from God back into prayer. The prayer never ceases!

**Contemplating (*contemplatio*):** The last step is the most difficult and rewarding. You have **read** the text, **studied** the text, **and prayed** the text. Now it is time to **be** the text. Let it seep into your being. Be still and listen. Make sure you leave some time after the prayer for silence and reflection. It is said that Dan Rather once interviewed Mother Theresa about her prayer life. Rather asked her, "What do you say to God when you pray?" Her answer was simple; "I don't say anything; I just listen." After that he asked, "Well, what does Jesus say to you?" And Mother Theresa answered, "Oh, He doesn't say anything, either. He just listens." Listening is what is important. You may not always feel anything, but God is there. Another facet of contemplation is to learn to *do* the text. We cannot be just hearers of the word; we must also be doers of the word. Let the scripture change the way you live your life.

## APPLYING THE PRINCIPLES IN PARTICIPATORY STUDY

### Preparation

As you begin the study, preparation will involve getting the materials you want to use, then prayer to begin each session of study. Part of this introductory time will be making decisions about the time and resources you can devote to this study. This is also your time of prayer. Before you begin to read, you need to pray. Then you need to listen. You come to the text because God calls you to it.

## OVERVIEW

Getting the overview is accomplished by reading the letters of John through at least once, but preferably three times. Don't feel bad about how many times you read. Choose a number that seems reasonable to you. If you start reading the third time, and it feels like a burden, move on. This is part of *lectio* but only part. You will learn to read in other ways in different phases of your study. Once you have read the letters of John through your chosen number of times, read one or two of the following

1.  The entry on the letters of John in a Bible handbook

2.  The entry on the letters of John in a Bible dictionary

3.  The introductory note on the letters of John in a study Bible, if you're using one.

4.  The introductory section of a good commentary on letters of John (see Appendix B for resource details)

Here is where we introduce historical elements into your study. Don't imagine that God cannot talk to you through this text because you are so far separated from the people who wrote it. They were people like you who had hopes, dreams, gifts, and failings. Study the background to help you connect to them. Christianity is a community that extends not only in space right now but in time.

## The Central Loop

For this overview, your central loop, as I call it, is your whole study of the book. Keep in mind that no element of your study is something you do just once and then forget about it. Prayer is continuous. There are multiple ways of reading, questioning, studying, and sharing.

For this study, I have divided the letters of John into eleven units.

- Introductory Matters—The Word of God and the Word of Life (1 John 1:1-4; John 1:1-18)

- Walking in the Light (1 John 1:5-2:6)

- A New Commandment (1 John 2:7-28)

- The Children of God (1 John 2:27-3:10)

- Love One another (1 John 3:11-24)

- Testing the Spirits (1 John 4:1-6)

- Behold the Love of God (1John 4:7-21)

- Overcoming the World (1 John 5:1-12)

- Prayers of Restoration (1 John 5:13-21)

- Walking in Obedience (2 John)

- Walking in Truth (3 John)

This is most closely related to *meditatio*, but the implementation of *meditatio* extends into the next section where you question the text in a directed way. Don't concentrate on the boundaries between one activity and the next. They are all related!

With each unit there will be an opportunity to try to think of new questions one might ask for further study. Generating new questions helps keep us from getting stale. Not only do I not have all the answers; I don't even have all the questions! Think of a question primarily as a way to prepare your mind to hear the text. When we listen or read, we often hear what we expect to hear. If I'm listening to the radio for weather, I may miss a major discussion of politics. You can miss what God is saying to you through a Bible writer because you are looking for something else. Questioning is an important part of *meditatio*, but it also relates closely to *oratio*— take your questions to God in prayer.

Finally, find something to share. Remember that sharing can be in the form of a question. For example, one might ask others how they understand a particular word, such as "incarnation," "poverty," or "atonement." Take notes on their answers, and bring that information back to your study. Then ask yourself what your neighbors will hear when you make particular statements, such as "I must be bold for Jesus!" or "Jesus is the only way to receive atonement." Do those statements mean something to them? Do they mean the same thing to them as they do to you?

This is part of *contemplatio*, as you try to be and do the text. We often think of sharing primarily as telling someone things that we have learned. But if what you learned is that God loves prisoners, for example, you might find that the best way of sharing that lesson is to become active in prison ministry. Sharing demonstrates that you don't believe the text is your private possession. It is God's gift to the Christian community.

## RESOURCES

The following resources are referenced regularly in the text. Additional resources are listed in the Appendix. In a small group it is a good idea to have different members of the group bring different reference works. For individual study, use a selection:

1. **Study Bibles.** There are a considerable number of study bibles available. Some take a more scholarly approach, while

others are devotional. In selecting a study bible, it is best to begin by selecting a specific translation and then find a study bible that is based upon that text. The New International Version is very popular and there are a large number of study bibles related to it. While the NIV emerged from evangelical Protestantism, most mainline Protestant churches use the New Revised Standard Version. If your choice is the NRSV (as is true for me) then the leading options are: *The New Oxford Annotated Bible, New Interpreter's Study Bible, The Harper-Collins Study Bible*, and *The Access Bible*. Again, these are not the only translations or study bibles available for consultation, especially since the ones mentioned are based on the New Revised Standard Version. A note on study bibles in general—one should be careful to separate in one's mind the text from the commentary. It is easy to confuse them since the two are placed together. It is, of course, always good to look at resources from a variety of perspectives, and thus resources beyond one's study bible should be consulted. Look at materials you are likely to disagree with to stimulate your thinking.

2.  **Concordances.** You may decide to consult either English language concordances, or those that include material on the original languages. If you get a concordance, find one that matches the Bible version you use. Besides print versions there are several free online sites that are helpful, including The Bible Gateway (multiple translations) and the Oremus Bible Browser (NRSV).

3.  **Bible Dictionaries.** The information in a good bible dictionary overlaps what is found in many study Bibles and Bible handbooks, but they can be very useful for general study of topics being considered. It is important that if purchasing a bible dictionary to get an up-to-date one. See the resource list for suggestions.

4. **Bible Handbooks.** The information found in a Bible handbook will be similar to what is found in many study Bibles, only it will lack the biblical text.

5. **Bible Commentaries**. These resources offer more detailed exegetical explanations and interpretation of the actual text. They range from one-volume to multiple volumes. For the New Testament, I would recommend purchase of *The People's New Testament Commentary* written by Fred Craddock and Eugene Boring. In purchasing commentaries, it is best to stay away from sets such as *Matthew Henry* or *Jameson, Fawcett, and Brown*. These were written several centuries ago and lack the kinds of historical and linguistic information you will need for deeper study. They can have some devotional value, but they can be found online.

When it comes to comparing passages, you will find your study Bible, concordance, and any Bible with reference notes to be very useful. Remember, however, that even the cross-references are just someone's opinion of how one passage is related to another. You don't have to agree. Look at the passages yourself, and ask not just whether they are related, but *how* they are related.

Remember to keep an open mind and a receptive heart while studying the Bible. Study prayerfully. Meditate on what you read. Try to place yourself in the audience of people who might have first heard this book read to them aloud in a small house church.

# SESSION 1

## INTRODUCTORY MATTERS— THE WORD OF LIFE

### VISION:

Participants will have the opportunity to address introductory matters, such as authorship, date, structure, and themes of the letters. They will also have the opportunity, to gain a sense of the core purpose of 1 John, by looking at the first four verses of the letter, and comparing this prologue with that of John 1:1-18.

### READING: 1 JOHN 1:1-4; JOHN 1:1-18

Please read the passage for the day in at least two different translations, a more formal translation, such as the NRSV, CEB, RSV, or NIV, and then read it again in a freer version or paraphrase such as *The Message*, *Phillip's*, or The *New Living Translation*. As you read pay attention to images that warrant further exploration. If you have access to the internet, Bible Gateway allows you to read the passage in parallel form.

### LESSON:

### Authorship and Context:

It is usually appropriate to begin an introductory lesson by looking at questions of authorship, context, and destination. When a piece of literature is supposed to be a letter, we look to the opening lines for some hint as to the identity of the author, as well as the identity of the recipient. We would also try to identify the context out of which the document emerged. The three letters attributed to a person named John pose difficulties in this regard. First, regarding the genre, while 2 and 3 John have the markings of a letter, the same cannot be said for 1 John. The first "letter" does not identify the author or context. Instead, it opens with a prologue (1 John 1:1-4), much like the Gospel of John. Therefore, while we will speak of this document as a letter, we do so cautiously.

Both 2 and 3 John will have their own chapters, at which time we will look more closely at the questions of authorship, date, genre, and context of those letters. I will note here, however, that these two "letters" do not offer much information as to the identity of the author, the recipient, or the date of its composing. The only identifier we find in the letters is the word "Elder" (Gk. *Presbuteros*). Regarding the date of their composition, the only letter with early attestation is 1 John. Questions continued to be raised about the authenticity of both 2 and 3 John as late as the fourth century.

Tradition has long linked these letters to the author of the Gospel of John, and the similarities in vocabulary and style are noticeable. There are differences as well. Whether they have the same author, there are sufficient similarities among the documents to assume that they form what some scholars have termed a "Johannine canon." That is, even if they do not share the same author, there are enough similarities to suggest that the Gospel and the Letters emerged out of the same community. As we progress through the letters, we will want to be alert to themes and ideas that are found both in the Gospel and the letters.

Despite the lack of either internal or external evidence for determining authorship, tradition has attributed the authorship of the Gospel and Letters to the Apostle John. The author of 2 and 3 John simply identifies himself as the *presbuteros* or elder, while 1 John remains a completely anonymous book. However, for the purposes of our study, we will refer to the author as John. This does not mean that I am taking a position on the identity of the author, it's simply easier to use this designation for the author.

Since we lack any identifying authorial marks in the letter, we can take note of its use by the early church. The earliest attestation of 1 John is found in Polycarp's "Letters to the Philippians," which offers echoes of what we read in 1 John. That evidence dates to around 135 CE. Eusebius records the words of Papias, who was active in the early second century, referring to the "former letter of John and that of Peter." What is intriguing, is if this is truly from Papias, it would precede any known reference to the Gospel of John. The next evidence comes around 180, when we find Irenaeus quoting from both 1 and 2 John in Against Heresies. In using these letters, Irenaeus attributes them to the son of Zebedee, the disciple of Jesus, and author of the Gospel. Thus, by the third century 1 John was considered an authoritative text. As for the letters, their status remained uncertain at best for some time. The first reference to 3 John does not appear until the mid-third century, and the scriptural status of both 2 and 3 were still being questioned in the fourth century.[2]

When it comes to the authorship of 1 John, questions center on its relationship to the Gospel. There are some signs that it could have been written prior to the Gospel, since the letter is less polished than the gospel and the theology seems to be more primitive than the Gospel. On the other hand, there are also signs of dependence on the Gospel by the letter writer. There is no definitive proof either way, but most scholars believe that the Gospel is prior to the letter. One possibility is that the letters depended on an earlier version of the Gospel, rather than the finished product. That would explain the letter's more primitive theology, as well as the signs of the letter's dependence on the Gospel. With that in mind, most scholars date the letter to around 100 CE, while the Gospel would have been written around 90 CE.

Not only is the authorship and date of composition uncertain, the same is true for the location of the receiving community. The connection with Polycarp, the earliest attestation, suggests that the letter emerged in Asia Minor or modern Turkey, though some

2   Judith Lieu, *I, II, III John (New Testament Library)*, (Louisville, KY: Westminster John Knox Press, 2008), kindle loc. 182-184.

scholars have suggested Palestine or Syria as a point of origin. Ultimately none of this can be verified.

There is a hint to the nature of the authorship with the word "we," and the reference to having seen and touched the Word of Life. That claim suggests a direct connection to Jesus, which would make sense if the author was the Apostle John. An alternative answer, and one that makes better sense of approximate date and possible context, is that the author(s) are the bearers of a tradition that has direct lineage to the Apostles and thus to Jesus. As Raymond Brown suggests, these would be companions of the Beloved Disciple who figures prominently in the Gospel of John. There have been objections to this idea, but it makes sense of the context, and for our purposes we will adopt this view.[3] For our purposes, we will speak of the author as being John the Elder (even if not the Apostle).

## Structure of 1 John

As we read through 1 John, we need to keep in mind its structure. We have already noted that 1 John lacks the traditional marks of a letter, but whether this is a traditional epistle, sermon, or an early theological essay, there is an undeniable structure present in 1 John. The author appears to be weaving proclamation with moral exhortation. At the same time, the letter seems to lack "a single, tightly reasoned line of argument."[4] This will make our exploration of the letter more complex and perhaps more interesting, for the issues at hand will weave back and forth. We see this complexity of structure in the way the theme of love interplays with John's concern about the threat of those he views as adversaries, people he doesn't always speak of lovingly. Indeed, he calls them anti-Christs (1 John 2:18). Although the structure and argument are complex,

3    Raymond Brown, *The Epistles of John (The Anchor Bible)*. (Garden City, NY: Doubleday and Company, 1983), p. 160.

4    C. Clifton Black, "The First, Second, and Third Letters of John," *New Interpreter's Bible: A Commentary in Twelve Volumes,* (Nashville: Abingdon Press, 1998), 12:371.

the author of 1 John appears to have in mind the basic message about Jesus found in the Gospel, that the Word has become flesh and dwelt among us (John 1:1, 14).

## The Adversaries

Reading through the letters, we discover that John the Elder is pushing back against adversaries who are undermining the community. It appears likely that these adversaries are people who had once been part of the community but had left it and were seeking to draw others out. Though, in 3 John reference is made to Diotrephes, who appears to remain within the community as an opponent to the author of the letter. The tenor of the arguments suggest that John believed that they threatened the survival of the community and needed to be stopped. As we proceed through the letter, we'll want to keep these adversaries in mind, as this will help us understand the apparent harshness that the one who proclaims the love of God shows to certain people. In recent decades, certain portions of the Christian community have focused attention on the rise of a person whom they identify as the "Anti-Christ." While the term "anti-Christ" appears only in the letters of John, the term has taken on a life of its own, being defined through other references to a world-ruling figure, but in the letters, the term is used more broadly for those who deny that Jesus is the Christ (1 John 2:18ff). Nonetheless, the references to anti-Christs appear in the context of a discussion of the end of days. That means, despite the delightful words about love and hospitality, these are polemical works. We may not fully know who these opponents are, but they are considered "armed and dangerous."

Among the issues that emerge are the nature of Christian hospitality and questions of authority in the community. Standing at the center of the conflicts that have emerged is the identity of Jesus. John's opponents may have held docetic or gnostic views of Jesus and were attempting to bring these views into the church, causing division and thus harm to the congregation. The opponents message appears to be that Jesus did not come in the flesh (2 John

7-9), contradicting the message of the community as found in the Gospel of John, which declared that the Word became flesh and dwelt among humanity (John 1:14). In the end, John faces an age-old problem, that of division and schism, which often creates a sense of hatred toward those with whom one disagrees.

## The Themes

Clifton Black suggests that readers keep in mind six primary themes that are present in the letters. First, there is the declaration that God is light (1 John 1:5). The second theme is the interpretation of the tradition the author has been expounding. The third theme is eschatological (unlike the Gospel, which demonstrates what is known as "realized eschatology," the letters speak of the imminent closing of the current age. This is, according to the author, the "last hour." The fourth theme has to do with Jesus becoming flesh. Continuing with Jesus, "he is the expiation for our sins." This is an important theme that will need some attention. The final theme is the one which we have come to identify with these letters and that is the call to love.[5] We will want to pay attention to each of these themes as we contemplate these letters.

## The Tradition: (1 John 1:1-4)

The Gospel of John starts with words that reflect the opening words of Genesis 1: "In the beginning." 1 John opens with: "We declare to you what was from the beginning." This usage is intriguing. The author of the letter wants the reader to go back to the beginning of things, though unlike the Gospel, the letter starts with the incarnation and not the creation. As with the Gospel, 1 John begins with a theological prologue. In this case, the prologue focuses on the tradition passed down to the community that reveals what the author(s) claim to have heard, seen, and touched. In the concern of the letter's author about beginnings, it is appropriate to recall what the Gospel had to say about beginnings. The Gospel opens with the declaration that "in the beginning was the Word,

5    Black, "First, Second, and Third Letters, of John," 12:374-376.

and the Word was with God, and the Word was God" (John 1:1). The author of the letter seems to pick upon this theme, for the author takes up that which has been heard, seen, and touched. The emphasis of the Gospel on the incarnation, on the embodied nature of Jesus, is picked up by the author of 1 John.

What the author claims to have heard, seen, and touched, is "the Word of life." The letter testifies to this Word (logos) that brings life, so that the readers might be in fellowship with the author (who has seen and touched this word), even as the author is in fellowship with the Father and the Son. Notice that while this is not a Trinitarian statement, it does suggest what some call a binatarian or dyadic relationship between Father and Son. Finally, this witness to the Word of Life, which leads to fellowship, is written so that the joy of the author might be complete. Whomever is the intended audience, the author is concerned about the state of their fellowship. They're concerned that members of the community have become disconnected to the tradition that goes back to Jesus, and they want to restore them to the right path (a theme that is present throughout the letter). This should give us some hints as to what we will encounter going forward. If fellowship has been broken, the question is how should it be restored?

John is concerned that the readers of this essay are in danger of becoming separated from the Word of Life, to which John bears witness. This reference to the Word of Life hearkens back to the declaration in the Gospel that the Word (Logos) is God (John 1:1), and incarnate in the person of Jesus (John 1:14). John wants to reconnect those who have gone astray to the tradition.

The author(s) declare what was from the beginning, that which they saw with their eyes and touched with their hands. As we've noted, the authors would not have been eyewitnesses, but in claiming to be witnesses to Christ's life and ministry they claim to be bearers of a tradition that goes back to the eyewitnesses. They are claiming for themselves the right to interpret the ministry of Jesus, so that all might be in fellowship with the Father and with the Son. This emphasis on seeing and touching is an important one for the community of John, because the adversaries we'll meet seem to deny the full meaning of the incarnation. The opponents, the ones who have departed the community, appear to take a docetic view of Jesus. The author(s) of the letter appear to claim that they are the correct or orthodox interpreters of the tradition passed down from the Beloved Disciple, that is the message of the Gospel of John. As Raymond Brown puts it: "The Prologue sets the tone for I John in terms of a polemically exclusive claim, namely, that the proclamation about Jesus made by the author represents the authentic Gospel stemming from a true witness to Jesus, and those who refuse to accept it have communion with neither the Father nor Son."[6]

This may be a theological polemic with Christological implications (did Jesus really have flesh?), but 1 John also has a practical focus. John is concerned about the nature of the fellowship (*koinōnia*) present in the community. The Gospel never uses this word, but it becomes important in the Letter. The issue here is two-fold—communion with God and communion with the congregation. The adversaries have broken fellowship with both God and congregation, causing a disruption in the community. The reason for the letter is restoration of communion with God and congregation, so that their joy may be restored.

## QUESTIONS FOR MEDITATION AND DISCUSSION:

1.  What do we know about the authorship and context of the Johannine letters? Does this make a difference in the way we approach these letters?

2.  Whether they share authorship, there seems to be a connection between the Gospel of John and the Letters. Both have theological prologues. Reading the Prologue of John (John 1:1-18), and comparing it with the Prologue of 1 John (1:1-4), what themes and words are found in the two Prologues? If we

---

6    Brown, *Epistles of John*, p. 175.

add in 1 John 1:5, does this add anything to the conversation about prologues? What do the similarities suggest?

3.   The Gospel of John starts with the declaration that in the beginning was the Word (Logos), which is God. It then declares that this Word became Flesh. In 1 John, we have reference to the Word (Logos) of Life. If we assume a dependence by the letter on the Gospel, what can we say about this "Word of Life?"

4.   What do you make of the author's insistence that the message they declare is one that was from the beginning, and that they have heard, seen, and touched the Word of Life? Without reading the remainder of the letter, what might these words suggest about the author's concerns?

5.   The author(s) speak of their desire to have fellowship with the reader. Do you sense in this that something is disrupting their fellowship/communion?

6.   Considering this word about fellowship/communion, what barriers to fellowship can emerge within a congregation? Why do these emerge? What can be done about them?

7.   The author(s) declare that their joy would be made complete if fellowship is restored. What is joy that we should desire it?

## EXERCISE:

While we speak of these three documents as letters of John, 1 John lacks traditional markers of a letter. To gain a better sense of what these markers are, find a Bible dictionary and read articles about epistles and letters. Then compare the opening and closing verses of the three letters of John with a Pauline letter such as 1 Corinthians or Galatians. Note the differences and keep them in mind as you continue reading the letters of John.

## A CALL TO PRAYER:

*As we go forth from this place, having shared in the light of God, may we carry that light into the world, so that God's grace might be revealed to all. Amen.*

# SESSION 2

## WALKING IN THE LIGHT

### 1 John 1:5-2:6

### VISION:

In this second session, we will dive more deeply into 1 John. We will want to keep in mind John's audience, including the adversaries. We noted in the opening session that this is a polemical work, even if it speaks of love. In this session, we are reminded that God is light and that those who walk with God will walk in the light. The opposite of the light is darkness, day and night, and so there is also a conversation about sin and its solution. The call here then is to walk in the light, even as God is light (a message found here and in the prologue to the Gospel of John—the light shines in the darkness (John 1:6).

### READING: 1 JOHN 1:5-2:6

Please read the passage for the day in at least two different translations, a more formal translation, such as the NRSV, CEB, RSV, or NIV, and then read it again in a freer version or paraphrase such as *The Message*, *Phillip's*, or The *New Living Translation*. As you read pay attention to images that warrant further exploration.

### LESSON:

**God Is Light (1 John 1:5)**

An ancient Easter hymn declares:

That Easter day with joy was bright,
the sun shone out with fairer light,
when, to their longing eyes restored,
the glad apostles saw their Lord.[7]

This first letter of John invites us to open our eyes and see the Lord. Having had our sight restored, we confess that "God is Light, and in him there is no darkness at all" (1 John 1:5). This confession that God is light, which has its parallels in the Gospel of John, declares that the Word is the Light that shines in the darkness, and the darkness does not overcome it (John 1:1-5). The confession that God is light should suggest various other biblical texts and images that can help us better understand who we are as the children of God. And there is no better place to start than at the beginning, where God says: "Let there be light" (Genesis 1:3). When God saw the light, God declares that the light was good.

John apparently assumes that we would all agree with his confession that God is light, because he goes right on and applies this confession to the lives of his readers. But before we skip to the application, it would be helpful to stop and think about what this confession means. When we read Eugene Peterson's translation of this text, the contrast appearing in this statement becomes a bit clearer. In *The Message*, God is described as "pure light" and "without a trace of darkness in him." God is pure and perfect light. There is no stain, no impurity. There isn't even a shadow. If God is pure light, without any darkness or shadow present, what does that mean? Could it mean that when it comes to God's nature no evil, deceit, or capriciousness is present? That would suggest that God can't be bribed or corrupted? Indeed, if this definition is true, then it's impossible to manipulate God or use God to justify our darker moments. Therefore, to walk with God is to walk in the light and not the darkness.

---

7    "That Easter Day with Joy Was Bright," *Chalice Hymnal*, (St. Louis: Chalice Press, 1995), 229

## Walking in the Light (1 John 1:6-10)

Beginning in verse six, we find the first of several "if-then" clauses. The question here concerns the link between our words and our deeds. So, "if we say" that we have communion (*koinonia*) with God, who is light, but walk in darkness, then, according to John, we lie, and we fail to do what is right. On the other hand, "if we walk in the light," then we have fellowship or communion with one another. It's important to note the contrast between saying and doing. As D. Moody Smith puts it, "to speak correctly but not to act correctly is fundamentally suspect and specious."[8] To put it in the vernacular, you should walk your talk. If all that you do is talk, then all you're doing is boasting.

When John goes through this series of clauses, he has in mind a certain group of people who have been boasting, and that is the adversary who had seceded from the community. It appears that these secessionists, believing they were holier than the community they left behind, have made certain claims, including being in communion with God. They also claim to be free from the guilt of sin. Finally, they claim they haven't sinned. According to John, none of these boasts are true. Therefore, the truth does not lie within them. Ultimately, due to their failure to recognize their own lies, they end up calling God a liar. As we progress through the letter, we will begin to see more clearly who and what these adversaries are.

While God might be pure light, without a trace of darkness, the same is not true of humanity. The question is: to what degree does darkness control one's life. John suggests that humans have a choice—we can decide whether we're going to walk in the light or in the darkness.

When I think of this choice between light and darkness, my thoughts are drawn to the *Star Wars* films. Although the way the films develop this idea is simplistic, there's something to be learned from them. The point that's made in the films is that our choices

---

8    D. Moody Smith, *First, Second, and Third John (Interpretation: A Bible Commentary for Teaching and Preaching)*, (Louisville: John Knox Press, 1991), p. 42.

color the way we live our lives. They also suggest that these choices aren't as easy as we might think. We'd all like to think that we're on the right side of things—that we're people of the light—but as we learn from the films, darkness has its attractions. There's a certain power that emerges from dark emotions like anger, hatred, and fear. But, if we give the reins of our lives over to these dark emotions, we may think that we are gaining power over the fates of ourselves and others, but in reality, we are turning control over to these dark emotions. Sometimes, we may even have good intentions, and believe that our choices are the right ones, and that they benefit others, but in the end, we discover that darkness has consumed us. This dilemma is well illustrated in decisions made by governments, even democratically elected governments, that are expressive of this darkness. Consider how, after 9-11, Justice Department lawyers gave the green light to the military and to the CIA to engage in torture—doing so in the name of protecting the nation's security.

Returning to the movies, the characters of Anakin and Luke Skywalker, father and son, live out the tension that exists between light and darkness. Anakin becomes powerful by tapping into his anger and his resentment, but in the end this power destroys the very people he loves. In the end, it consumes him—turning him into Darth Vader. Luke on the other hand, although tempted by the possibilities of the dark side, especially when he's offered the opportunity to save friends and loved ones, chooses to walk in the light. By embracing the light, he takes a risk, but in the end, he redeems his father and saves his friends and loved ones.

If there's unwelcome news here, there's also good news. First the bad news. According to John, it's quite likely that we've not broken free from sin's hold on our lives. He tells the readers the unwelcome truth: "if we say that we have no sin, we deceive ourselves" (vs. 8). Because the adversaries would not make a confession of their sins, they deceived themselves. This if clause is followed by another one. Here is the good news—the light is stronger than the darkness. That process begins with confession of sin. John writes that "if we confess our sins, He who is reliable and just will forgive us our sins and cleanse us from all wrongdoing" (vs. 9).[9] The sinner has a part to play in reconciliation. There is need for confession. However, that confession rests on the reliability or faithfulness of the one who forgives. It does us little good to confess sins, if there is no hope of forgiveness. Thus, God is reliable, but God is also just.

## Christ is our Advocate (1 John 2:1-2)

When Darkness gets control of us—which it does on occasion— John says that God provides an antidote. This divinely provided way of redemption and renewal sets us free from the whirlpool of darkness. While John hopes we will not sin, he also understands that it's quite likely that we will sin. When we sin, God provides an Advocate, Jesus Christ the Righteous, to serve as mediator. Jesus makes it possible for Christians, even the entire world, to stand before God and bask in God's glory. As Beverly Gaventa puts it: "The fellowship of Christians then is not a fellowship of those who do not sin; but a fellowship of those who know that they have Jesus as their advocate when they sin."[10]

If we are to walk in the light, we must take stock of the darkness—the sin—present in our lives. It is important that we recognize that all sin, falling short of God's vision for humanity. At the same time, it is also important we remember that this darkness needn't define who we are. John writes to the churches with whom he is connected, hoping to guide them toward a way of living that isn't defined by the darkness of sin. John is realistic enough to know that there is a tendency to fall into sin. Therefore, "if anyone does sin, we have an advocate with the Father." This advocate is Jesus, who according to John, is righteous. Since we need to pay attention to terms appearing both in the Gospel and the letters, the word Advocate should stand out. The Greek word here is *paraklētos*. It occurs several times in the Farewell Discourse found in John 14-

9   Translation made by Raymond E. Brown, *The Epistles of John (The Anchor Bible)*, (Garden City, NY: Doubleday and Company, 1982), p. 191.

10  Beverly Gaventa in *Texts for Preaching. Year B: A Lectionary Commentary Based on the NRSV*, Beverly Gaventa, Ed., (Louisville: Westminster John Knox Press, 1993), 283.

15. In the Gospel *paraklētos* is used in reference to the Holy Spirit. Here in 1 John, *paraklētos* is used in reference to Jesus and his work. While this Greek word can be translated in several ways, the most common translation of the word in 1 John is advocate. The sense of the use here is that Jesus serves as our defense attorney, standing before God, arguing on our behalf. It is also possible to use the word intercessor here, or we could follow Eugene Peterson who translates *paraklētos* as priest-friend. This is an interesting phrase, which offers some possibilities. If we follow Peterson, we might interpret John in light of the reference in the book of Hebrews to Jesus serving as our high priest, intervening with God on our behalf (Hebrews 4:4-6). This might be what Peterson has in mind here.

Whether Jesus is our defense attorney or priest, he is the one who intercedes with God on our behalf. It is in this capacity that Jesus serves as the "atoning sacrifice" for our sins and the sins of the entire world (*kosmos*). This is the world, which according to the Gospel of John, God loved so much that God sent the Son into the world (John 3:16). When we encounter passages that speak of atonement, we need to pause and consider how the original authors and recipients would have understood the concept. Too often we read back into scripture theological ideas that emerged much later, and which may not fit this context. The Greek word translated here as "atoning sacrifice" (NRSV) is *hilasmos*. It has several possible meanings and uses, so we're left wondering what John has in mind.

It would be useful to note that when it comes to atonement theology, the Gospel of John does speak of Jesus being the paschal lamb, but it doesn't refer directly to a sacrifice. So, if the letters have a connection with the Gospel, what might the author of the letter have in mind when using this word? Is John thinking in terms of Jesus as a penal substitution, dying in our place, paying the price we owe for our sins? Or is something else going on here? One clue might be found in Jewish literature, which speak of the intercession of the martyrs, whose blood was being shed on behalf of the people (2 Maccabees 12:39-45). Consider the prayer of Eleazar as he was being tortured to death:

> 28 *"Have mercy on your people. Make our punishment sufficient for their sake. 29 Purify them with my blood, and take my life in exchange for theirs." 30 When he said this, the holy man died with dignity from the torture. By thinking clearly, he resisted even while facing the pains of death for the sake of the Law.* (4 Maccabees 6:28-29 CEB).

Since *hilasmos* can be rendered as atonement, but it can also be translated as expiation, propitiation, remedy for defilement, and sacrifice for sin, what does John have in mind in this case?

Is Jesus placating an angry God (propitiation) or making us pure before God (expiation)? One thing we should note is that nowhere in this passage is the wrath of God mentioned. Clifton Black suggests that the emphasis here is not an act of turning away God's anger, but rather addressing human rebellion. Thus, "expiation is not a human maneuver that changes God from furious to loving; expiation is an expresson of God's love, which removes sin from the sinner."[11] For John, this act is universal in its scope. Might then Jesus be interceding, as Eleazar seems to be, on our behalf, based on his martyrdom, so that the people might be washed clean from their sins and restored to proper fellowship? There is another clue. Origen, writing in the third century, suggested that John is referring to the Jewish celebration of the Day of Atonement, which included sacrifices, but did not placate God's wrath. Instead, the atoning sacrifice served as a witness to the way in which Jesus cleansed the world of its sin. Jesus does this from the cross as our intercessor and attorney.

---

11   C. Clifton Black, "The First, Second, and Third Letters of John," *New Interpreter's Bible: A Commentary in Twelve Volumes,* (Nashville: Abingdon Press, 1998), 12:388.

## WALKING IN OBEDIENCE

Having been washed clean in the blood of Jesus, John calls on the reader to walk in obedience to God. To know God is to obey God. In a world that values freedom, a call to obedience may seem out of place. It belongs to another era, one that wasn't defined by democratic values. According to John, however, if you say you know God, but do not obey God's commandments, you are a liar. Belief requires action, if it is to be rendered true. Thus, if you obey God's word (logos), then the love of God reaches its perfection in you. To abide with him is to walk with him, and that involves obedience to him.

John speaks here of "knowing" God. The word "know" in some form is prominent in the Gospel of John and in this letter (twenty-five times in 1 John). That may have something to do with Semitic understandings of what it means to know something or someone. It is more than an intellectual understanding. It is experiential as well, which is why it has the meaning of sexual intimacy. Thus, as Raymond Brown puts it: "to know God means to share His life." That is also what is meant by the call to abide in Jesus and in God. Therefore, "sharing God's life means living according to His will, and so by keeping His commandments one comes to know Him intimately."[12] To claim an intimate relationship with God and not behave accordingly is to live a lie.

To truly know God is to abide in God, and that involves walking as Jesus walked. It involves trust—trust that Jesus knows the way. It also involves a renewing of one's life. In the Hebrew Bible, we see references to the law being written on the heart (Jer. 31:31), so that one no longer needs to be taught the law[13], for it will be imprinted on the heart. Again, turning to Raymond Brown: "Those who 'keep' God's commandments are acting according to the Spirit that God has put into their hearts, indeed according to

12    Brown, *Epistles of John*, p. 279.
13    Brown, *Epistles of John*, p. 280.

the new hearts (or natures) that God gave them when He begot them from above as His children."

So, what are the commandments of God? At this point the commandments haven't been explicitly stated, though the reader would likely know what is intended. As we move forward in John, we will encounter the commandment to love, but even here love has come to the fore, as John speaks of the person in whom the love of God has reached perfection (vs. 5). Here, for the first time in 1 John, we have the Greek word *agapē*. Here in 1 John, that love is understood as "a spontaneous, unmerited, creative love flowing from God to the Christian, and from the Christian to fellow Christian."[14] That love reaches its perfection when we abide in God's presence. That is our calling—to abide in Christ and walk in his ways.

## QUESTIONS FOR MEDITATION AND DISCUSSION:

1. We began this session with the declaration that "God is light and in him there is no darkness at all." If we compare this statement with the prologue to the Gospel of John (John 1:4-5), what do these statements suggest about God? What are the properties of light that might help us understand this statement about God?

2. Having declared that God is light, what are the implications of the call to walk in the light? What is the opposite of light and what would that look like? Could the imagery from Star Wars provide some insight?

3. The word "if" appears several times in the passage, including six times in verses 6-10 of chapter 1. What sense do you get from this usage? What is John trying to get across to us?

4. In the first session, looking at 1 John 1:1-4, John speaks of being in fellowship or communion (*koinonia*) with God and

---

14 Brown, *Epistles of John*, p. 255.

with the rest of the community. In this passage, why might John declare that those who claim to be in fellowship with Jesus but walks in darkness be lying? Why might the truth not be in them? Do you get the sense that problems are brewing in this community?

5.  When it comes to sin, which is an issue in this passage, why would we deceive ourselves if we claim that sin does not reside in us?

6.  Granting that sin resides in us, or that we sin, what is the remedy? (vs. 9). What does the image of cleansing suggest?

7.  Moving on into chapter 2, John writes that he would love it if they didn't sin—but remember that we all sin—what is the remedy for sin as expressed in 1 John 2:1-2?

    A. How is Jesus our advocate? How might the use of *paraklētos* in John 14-15 regarding the Spirit, help us understand what John has in mind here?

    B. What does it mean for Jesus, our advocate, to be the atoning sacrifice (*hilasmos*)?

    C. Is Jesus placating God's wrath (propitiation), or gaining God's attention so that God might wash away our sins (expiation)?

8.  Having spoken of a remedy sin, so that the people of God might be restored to fellowship, John moves to obedience. To know God is to obey the commandments. How might obedience be a sign of relationship to God?

    A. Why might John focus on obedience as a sign of relationship?

    B. Why would disobedience, or failure to walk in the ways of God, be a sign of darkness? Again, do you see signs of division within the community? Why might divisions be considered sin?

9.  The passage for the day closes with John declaring that "whoever says, 'I abide in him' ought to walk as he walked." What might John have in mind here?

    A. What does it mean to abide in him?

    B. In answering this question, consider how the word is used in the Gospel of John—such as in John 15:1-10, where Jesus speaks of the vine and branches. How might this reading from the Gospel help us understand what is meant here?

## EXERCISE:

The reference here to Jesus being the "atoning sacrifice" raises questions about God and our relationship to God. While the cross is not mentioned directly in this passage, using a concordance or dictionary look up passages in the New Testament where the Greek word hilasmos are found. How is this word used in Hebrews or in the Pauline epistles to speak of Jesus? Does it carry the idea of propitiation (placating God's anger) or expiation (cleansing) or some other meaning? Is this different or like how the word is used in 1 John?

## A CALL TO PRAYER:

*May we who seek to walk in the light of God, having been set free from bondage to sin through Christ's actions on the cross, live out our claim to love God through acts of love and grace in the world.*

# SESSION 3

## A NEW COMMANDMENT

### 1 John 2:7-28

VISION:

Many know 1 John for its proclamation that God is love. Here in chapter 2, John speaks of a new command to love, but does in the context of expanding divisions. John seeks to identify the challenges facing the community, which have a Christological focus, writing to encourage the community to hold to the truth and to each other, thus expressing the vision of love.

READING: 1 JOHN 2:7-28

Please read the passage for the day in at least two different translations, a more formal translation, such as the NRSV, CEB, RSV, or NIV, and then read it again in a freer version or paraphrase such as *The Message, Phillip's,* or the *New Living Translation.* As you read, pay attention to images that warrant further exploration:

LESSON:

### New Commandments and Old (2:7-11)

John writes about a new commandment, that in reality is not new but is rather old. While this sounds confusing, John appears to want the community to remember a command that they had known from the beginning. It is important to remember that John (whoever John is) wants his community to hold fast to what was delivered to them in the beginning. That is, what had been heard, seen, and touched, "concerning the word of life" (1 John 1:1).

What he wants them to remember is not something new in terms of age (*neos*), but in terms of freshness (*kainos*). As to the identity of this commandment, the most likely explanation is that John is referring to the New Commandment Jesus gave on the night prior to his death. In John 13, Jesus gives a "new commandment, that you love one another. Just as I have loved you, you also should love one another" (John 13:34). The giving of this new command to love one's neighbor is found as well in the Synoptic Gospels, though at a different point in the story. In Matthew's version, Jesus is in a conversation with the Pharisees, and suggests that the command to love one's neighbor, along with the command to love God are the foundation for the message of the Law and Prophets (Matthew 22:34-40; Mark 12:28-34; Luke 10:25-28).

This old but fresh commandment is issued to a community that is experiencing division, but John assures them that the light (Jesus) is shining and the darkness is passing away. Yes, the true light is beginning to shine. There is a clear eschatological element here. The darkness would appear to be the world as it has been. This old world is passing away, and a new world order is beginning to take shape. John makes a practical observation here. Using the light/darkness contrast, he declares that one cannot say "I am the light" and then hate one's brother or sister. If you give in to hate, you live in darkness. Again, I'm drawn back to the *Star Wars* analogy—the Emperor made clear that if you embrace hate, you embrace the dark side of the Force. Yes, there is much power to be found in hate, but it is not the way of God. Having made note of this, we will need to be aware of how John speaks of love and hate. Context here is important. Is his focus on the internal workings of the community or the world at large?

The word we hear in verse 10 concerning loving a brother or sister draws on Jesus' new commandment to love another (John 13:34), so that "whoever loves a brother or sister (*adelphoi*) lives in the light." Now the question emerges, who are the brothers and sisters that one is to love? In context, it is likely that John has in mind members of the Beloved Community, and not those outside the community. That is, the command to love, as expressed in this letter, is addressed only to the Johannine community. This may help explain John's sometimes harsh rhetoric about his opponents and the world at large. He suggests that those who abandon the community are not worthy of love. There is no call to love one's neighbor or one's enemy. There is only a call to love one's *adelphoi* (brother or sister). Since, the love command is issued at the Last Supper to a rather select group of people, this only solidifies this view. The question then becomes whether this more exclusive vision of community should hold true going forward, or is it a product of an early stage of development?

The context of the letter is important, especially if we're going to understand what John means when writing about love and hate. It is clear that the community is experiencing division or schism, and doctrine seems to be at the heart of the debate (thus heresy?). Addressing the matter of hate, and how it relates to living in darkness, John is clear that this hate is hurting the community. D. Moody Smith writes:

> One has the impression of a sea of hatred, in which the Johannine community exists as an island of love, beleaguered and even betrayed. In the very nature of the case, love must be focused inward, for outside the community it is rejected.[15]

With former members of the community undermining the community (hating it), it seems that John is calling for the community to circle the wagons and make love for one another their primary commitment. This is a call to separate from the broader culture/society and create a counter-culture rooted in the tradition passed on to them by those who had been with Jesus in the beginning.

---

15  D. Moody Smith, *First, Second, and Third John (Interpretation)*, Louisville: Westminster John Knox Press, 1991), p. 61.

## Love not the things of the World (2:12-17)

The words of John 3:16 are well-known. We see the reference emblazoned on signs seemingly everywhere. "God so loved the *World* that he gave his only begotten Son . . ." If God loves the world, then shouldn't we love the world? That has been a constant theme in some circles, but what does John mean by it? In the Gospel of John, we learn that God provided a way for the world—the *kosmos*—to be redeemed through belief/trust in the Son. When John speaks of God's love of the world, which differs from a believer loving the world. John makes this clear in telling the reader not to "love the world or the things of the world," because "the love of the Father is not in those who love the world" (2:15). While God loves the cosmos, but we are not to love the world, which doesn't know God, does the command of Jesus to love our neighbors—a command not found in the Gospel or letters of John—can we, living in a different context, expand the circle of love. If God loves the cosmos, might we participate in that love? Or is there something so inherently dark present in the world as it stands, that we must completely separate ourselves from this world?

John's concern is for the community and its survival. There are people who were once part of the community who have left the community and are intent on bringing the rest of the community with them. John writes this letter to warn the community to stay clear of those who walk in darkness. John speaks of love but does so in the context of a light/darkness dualism that is prominent throughout the letters. Whatever John means by love, is understood in this context.

Moving on to verse 12, John issues a series of directives that seem repetitive but likely are written in a way to reinforce the message. He addresses the children, the fathers, and the young people, offering specific directions. To the children is given a reminder that their sins have been forgiven (vs. 12). To the fathers (if spiritual fathers are envisioned, can we not also speak of spiritual mothers?), is issued a reminder that they have known "him who is from the beginning" (vs. 13). Who is this one who is from the beginning? If we keep the Gospel ever in front of us, the one who is from the beginning is the Word (John 1:1). Regarding the identity of this group, it is intriguing that Eugene Peterson, in *The Message,* speaks of "veterans," incorporating both male and female disciples. John then writes to the young people because they have conquered the evil one. This is a most interesting statement, which deserves to be unpacked further. Could it be that the younger or new members of the community are on the front lines of this battle for the heart of the community? Are the adversaries targeting them? Having issued these directives the first time, John begins again. To the children, because they know the Father, to the fathers, because they know the one who is from the beginning, and then again there is a word to the young people. He writes to them because they are strong, "and the word of God abides" in them, so that they have overcome the evil one. Why are the "young people" being addressed in this way? How is it that they have remained strong in this battle? How is the word of God abiding in them?

As to the identity of the "young people," the Greek word here is translated most directly as "young men," but in the interest of inclusion, the NRSV uses young people, while *The Message* translates *neaniskoi* as "newcomers." The translators of the NRSV have chosen to use age categories in their translation, while Peterson has chosen to go with levels of spiritual maturity. Both are possible, though the simplest translation suggests going with age. Nonetheless there is another possibility. That would be that all disciples are children, who are divided into two groups—Fathers (veterans) and Young People (neophytes).

Whomever is understood to exist under the category of Young People, they are understood by John to have "conquered the evil one." In the second round, we see a further clarification. They have overcome or conquered the evil one because the "Word of God" abides in them. Considering the community context, the reference to the Word of God could go back to the Prologue of John's Gospel, which declares that the Word (*logos*) is God and became flesh and dwelt among us (John 1:1, 14). However, Raymond Brown suggests that this word is the commandment to love one's brother (and sister), as was revealed in verses 5-11. He points us to the words of Psalm 119:9: "How can a young man (*neōteros*) keep his way pure? By guarding it according to Your words (*logos*)"[16] Those who are young have stayed the course, and overcome the Evil One, because they have heeded the commandment of Jesus. Note the use once again of the word *abide.* This is an important Johannine word, signifying the importance of remaining connected to God through Jesus, and thus to the community that God has called together. As for the identity of the Evil One, we will learn more as we move forward, but it seems clear that John has in mind the devil. Thus, abiding in the word/commandment enables them to conquer the devil.

With this as a prelude, we come to John's seemingly incongruous demand that as a community we should not love the world or the things of the world. This is because the love of the Father is not with those who love the world. Even though God might love the cosmos, the cosmos might be problematic for the community, because the cosmos is marked by "the desire of the flesh, the desire of the eyes, the pride in riches," none of which comes from God. Essentially this is a warning against worldliness, of allowing the broader culture to define who the community is. The danger is reading this in a pietistic/puritanical way, so that we interpret the text to discourage card-playing, movie-going, and the like. It's possible that John would discourage these activities, but we simply do not know. The point is that the members of the community should avoid activities that undermine the community, that allow for incursions of darkness into a community of light. What we must avoid here is pitting the spiritual against the material. Rather as D. Moody Smith suggests, what is condemned here is "placing things—material, mental, or spiritual—in the position of ultimate object of desire." It is a warning against choosing what is transitory

---

16  Raymond Brown, *The Epistles of John (The Anchor Bible),* Garden City,
    NY: Doubleday and Company, 1982, p. 306.

over what is permanent, and that is salvation through Christ.[17] The call here is not to embrace a narrow piety, but to focus on what is most important, what is ultimate, and that is God. Or, as John puts it, "the world and its desire are passing away, but those who do the will of God live forever" (vs. 17).

## The coming of the Anti-Christ (18-28)

Having commended those who didn't embrace the desires of the World, but abided in the word or commandment of God, John then issues a warning about those who would entice the community to follow the way of darkness. It is in this section of 1 John that we begin to discern the nature of the sin that is upsetting the community. For the first time, John uses the term *antichrist*. In fact, the term *antichrist* only appears in 1 John. Modern readers of this passage will likely have been influenced by a popularization of an apocalyptic world view, which suggests that *the* Antichrist, a supernatural figure, will emerge at the end of the age in opposition to Jesus, leading to Armageddon and the end of the world. While John speaks of *antichrist,* he does so in both a singular and a plural form. It seems clear that he isn't thinking of a supernatural figure who will rule the world. Instead, these *antichrists* are people who have been members of the community, but who left the community and threaten its survival. This is a localized message that takes place under the backdrop of a cosmic battle between light and darkness.

This idea of a cosmic battle between light and darkness, between God and the devil, seems passé to many modern Christians, especially more progressive/liberal Christians. Having embraced the scientific values of the Enlightenment, we have disenchanted the world. Everything has a scientific explanation—or does it? As Richard Beck points out:

> We're living in an increasingly modern, scientific, technological, and therefore more skeptical age. Faith is harder for us. Doubt fills our pews . . . Many Christians

17  Smith, *First, Second, and Third John,* p. 66.

are losing their belief in God, so when you look at the
To-Do-List of Belief, endorsing the existence of the Prince
of Darkness seems pretty far down the list.[18]

It is easy to discount and skip over this section of 1 John, and
get to the good stuff, the stuff about loving one another. Neverthe-
less, John makes it clear that he and his community are engaging in
spiritual warfare. Richard Beck, who is a psychologist, and therefore
knows how the mind works, has discovered in the course of his own
life and ministry, including his psychological practice, that there is
a spiritual dimension to life that require a spiritual response.

This section of the letter begins with an apocalyptic declaration. This "is the last hour!" When we think about the connection
between the Gospel and the Letter, one of the distinguishing marks
is the Letter's more apocalyptic tone. The Gospel is understood to
offer a "realized eschatology." The realm of God runs parallel to this
age, without the kind of definitive marker between ages, which is
prominent in the Synoptic Gospels and in Paul. This is one of the
reasons why some believe the Letter predates the Gospel. It seems
more akin to the earlier Pauline emphasis that the end of the age
is near at hand, while the Gospel of John offers us a more "realized
eschatology." In the Gospel it seems that the community is settling
in for the long haul.

According to John, the marker that the last hour has arrived
is the coming of the antichrist, suggesting that the community
expected a figure to emerge who would threaten the community.
In fact, there experience is one of encountering many antichrists
(vs. 18). Who are the antichrists? They are the ones who "went out
from us, but they did not belong to us" (vs. 19). That is, they are the
ones who had disrupted the community by leaving it, taking with
them those whom they had deceived. In John's mind, those who
left, or at least led the exodus from the community, had never really
part of the community. They were interlopers, who entered the

---

18   Richard Beck, *Reviving Old Scratch: Demons and the Devil for Doubters
     and the Disenchanted,* (Minneapolis: Fortress Press, 2016), p. xv.

community only to create confusion. Looking back to the previous section, these are the ones who did not abide in God's command to love, but instead chose darkness and thus hated the members of the community. If they had belonged the community, then they would have stayed.

To this point we have held off on identifying the "sin" that the author of 1 John is concerned about. It seems clear here that the sin that has marred the community is *schism.* The antichrists are those individuals who separated themselves from the main body. It is this group of secessionists who have not only separated themselves from the community but have embraced darkness. They have allowed the Evil One to conquer them, through enticements of the world. They have loved the world, and the things of the world, so the Father is not in them.

John moves back and forth between those in the community and those who have left the community. In verses 20-21, he returns to those who have remained faithful, those who were "anointed by the Holy One," and who have the appropriate knowledge. Those who remained faithful are the ones who know the truth. They also know that no lie comes from the truth. To put it in modern parlance, there are no "alternative facts". As to the nature of this anointing, there is no clear answer. Scholars take different views on this, ranging from spiritual to material anointing. The word translated in the NRSV as anointing, *chrisma,* is a noun and not a verb. With that in mind, we might read this as addressing those who received the oil of anointing from the Holy One. The question is, to what effect? It could have been oil used in a physical ritual or it could be used in a figurative fashion. It's possible that John has in mind an initiation ceremony, such as baptism, which included anointing with oil. That was common in the early church, with the oil signifying the Holy Spirit. Or it could be seen metaphorically regarding the coming of the Spirit, whether it accompanied something material or not. In this case, he would be addressing a community that had been filled with the Holy Spirit and thus able to discern the truth. As to the identity of the Holy One, this could be the Holy Spirit, or it could be Jesus. Scholars simply are not of one mind on this. Raymond Brown summarizes the various questions, suggesting that the best way to read this verse is to see John "referring to an *anointing with the Holy Spirit,* the gift *from Christ* which constituted one a Christian."[19] Whether physical or not the reference to the anointing likely is connected to one's entry into the community, and it is this community that is of concern to John.

The word "knowledge" also is prominent in the letter. The secessionists are claiming to possess a certain form of spiritual knowledge they wish to offer to the community, but John stands in the gap, warning that the community, not the secessionists possess true knowledge. As those who know the truth, they also know that "no lie comes from the truth." What the secessionists offer is "fake news," a form of knowledge that deceives. Since the community knows the truth, the opponents are purveyors of lies.

So, how can one tell the difference between those who have the truth and those who are purveyors of lies? In verse 22, John tells us that a liar denies Jesus is the Christ. In the Gospel the opponents seem to be the "Jews," who appear frequently as opponents of Jesus. In that context, the animus toward the "Jews" may be rooted in the rising tensions between the Jewish community and an increasingly Gentile church.[20] In this case the separation seems to have already occurred, so the accusation that the opponents deny that Jesus is the Christ isn't a Jewish charge. It is true that the Jewish community denied that Jesus was the Messiah (*Christos*), which led to the expulsion of the followers of Jesus from the synagogues, but this appears to be an intra-community debate focused on doctrinal questions about the identity of Jesus. The question tips on the axis of the humanity/divinity of Jesus. More specifically, the focus seems to be on the humanity of Jesus. That is why the letter begins by citing the tradition that had been passed down from those who heard, saw,

---

19  Brown, *Epistles of John,* p. 348.
20  On the "Jews" in the Gospel of John, see Jaime Clark-Soles book *Reading John for Dear Life: A Spiritual Walk with the Fourth Gospel,* (Louisville: Westminster John Knox Press, 2016), pp. 155-162.

and touched Jesus. The secessionists appear to elevate the divinity of the Christ to a level that eliminated the humanness of Jesus. Thus, the adversaries were advocating a docetic Christology, which denied or denigrated the human part of the incarnation. They would have read the Johannine tradition in such a way as to push the witness to divinity to its furthest extent, crowding out the human side of the incarnation. This is why John calls them the antichrist. They deny the tradition of Jesus being the Christ, and in doing so they also the relationship of Father and Son. Therefore, if you deny the Son, including his humanity, you deny the Father. You can't have one without the other, and apparently the adversaries had tried to separate out the two. They have concluded that Jesus cannot be the Christ or the Son of God. But to do so is to act contrary to the Gospel. It's a false reading or interpretation, and by adopting it they have separated themselves from the community and have begun to walk in darkness.

The remedy here is to abide in the message that the community had received from the beginning. Stay away from new and deceptive ideas and doctrines. Hold fast to that which they had learned. This is a very conservative perspective. In that context, the word *abide* appears once again—if you abide in the Son, who is the human Jesus, and in the Father, you will experience eternal life.

John comes back in verses 26 and 27 with a word of encouragement in the face of incursions that were meant to deceive them. Since they have received the oil of anointing "from him who abides in you," they didn't need a teacher. They had the knowledge they needed, because what they need to know has been with them from the beginning. The second reference to anointing, when connected to teaching, suggests that whatever anointing took place, it was accompanied by catechetical instruction. The truth had already been shared, and therefore they need not adopt the new teaching being offered by the opponents, teaching that contradicted what they had been taught at the beginning. Apparently, the adversaries, whom John suggests are antichrists, were opposing the teaching of John and his colleagues, which had been revealed from the beginning, was Christological in nature.   Remembering that this is the "last hour," and that the expected antichrists have come, seeking to entice believers to break away from the community, it is clear that the warning against teachers here is a warning against following false prophets. Interestingly, John goes to the other extreme and warns against teachers, suggesting they are not needed. This could be taken as an expression of anti-intellectualism, which has reared its head on a regular basis throughout Christian history.

Our passage concludes in verse 28, with a call to abide in Christ, so that they might not "draw back in shame from him at his coming" (Brown, p. 378). The message here is one of encouragement. If they continue to abide in Jesus, then they'll have confidence on the day of his return. That eschatological/apocalyptic element is present here, but the word they hear is that they needn't worry about the future. Eternal life is assured, if they hold fast to what they had been taught from the beginning.

## QUESTIONS FOR MEDITATION AND DISCUSSION:

1.  As we begin this next section of 1 John, the author speaks in verses 7-8 of a new command, that really isn't new. If, as is thought, the reference goes back to the mandate in John 13:34, that we are to love one another, what does it mean to love one another as Christ has loved us?

    A. Who does Jesus, and by extension the author of this letter, have in mind here? Whom are we to love?

    B. How does the references to light and darkness influence the way we understand this commandment to love?

2.  In verses 9-11, we see John speak of light and darkness, of love and hate. How does light and darkness relate to love and hate? How does living in the light prevent one from stumbling and thus hating brothers and sisters? In this dualism, do you

see some form of separation taking place in the Christian community?

3. Moving into the next section, John tells the community that they cannot love the world or the things of the world. How does this statement fit with the words of John 3:16, which are well known to many—God loved the world so much that he gave his only son for the world? What might it mean for us not to love the world or the things of the world? (vs. 15)

4. As we ponder these questions, let us step back and take in verses 12-14. In these verses, John addresses three groups—children, fathers, and young people. While scholars are uncertain about whom is being addressed, what do you see here in these two sets of statements? What is John trying to accomplish? Do you see in these declarations a message that makes sense of the call of John not to love the world?

5. In his comments on verses 15-17, D. Moody Smith suggests that John is concerned about "placing things—material, mental, or spiritual—in the position of ultimate object of desire." How tempting is it to put the transitory above the permanent, and what does that say about the nature of the Christian faith?

6. When we reach verse 18, we're confronted with the declaration that this is the "Last Hour," which is marked by the coming of the antichrist. As you read this, what do you hear in this statement? What message do these words and phrases— "last hour" and "antichrist" —suggest?

7. We have been talking about the sin that John is concerned about, and in verse 19, we might get our first clue. What do you hear in John's statement that "they went out from us, but they did not belong to us?" Do you hear in this the sin of *schism*? If so, how is schism a sin? Should we even speak of schism in our day?

8.  In verses 20-21, John writes of an anointing by the Holy
    One, and of knowledge that they already have. Having been
    anointed, in some fashion, they have the truth. They also know
    that there is no truth in a lie. So, what is truth? What is John
    concerned about here, in light of what we've already learned?

9.  When we get to verse 22-23, we get more information about
    what is happening in John's community. Having been told that
    there are antichrists opposing the community, John speaks of
    the message of the liar. The antichrist denies that Jesus is the
    Christ. What might this mean? What is going on here?

    A.  Remember that unlike in the Gospel of John this isn't a
        conflict with Jews, it's a conflict that began within the
        Christian community. How might the adversaries have
        denied that Jesus is the Christ?

    B.  How might they, in doing this deny the Son and the
        Father?

10. In verses 24-25, John again uses the word "abide." He speaks
    of letting what they had heard from the beginning abide in
    them? What do you hear in this admonition, and why does
    abiding in this teaching lead to eternal life?

11. The concern here seems to be that the adversaries, those who
    had left the community, might deceive the believers with new
    teaching. What do you make of this statement that having
    been anointed they no longer needed teachers? What does
    this say about the anointing? Could John have in mind the
    catechetical instruction that normally accompanied baptism?

12. The section concludes with a word of encouragement in verse
    28. Why might abiding in Jesus provide confidence on the
    day of his return?

13. Looking back over this entire section, what do you hear? What
    message might it have for us?

## EXERCISE:

The word antichrist appears only in 1 John. However, this word has taken on a certain life of its own. Using a bible dictionary or other resources, look up other similar terms that appear in other passages. Have a conversation about what you have learned about these other terms and how they might influence the way we read this passage?

## A CALL TO PRAYER:

*Help us, O God, to hold fast to that which is good and true, that we might walk in your ways and live out that faith in ways that bless the community.*

# THE CHILDREN OF GOD

1 John 2:29-3:10

## VISION:

Even as the Gospel of John speaks of being born again or born from above, the letter talks about the community being children of God. The question is, what does John have in mind when he speaks of the community in this way? How does being a child of God differ from being a child of the devil? In that context, inviting discernment, John speaks of sin and lawlessness. His belief is that a child of God will not sin. So what is sin? That is one of the questions we wrestle with in this session.

## READING: 1 JOHN 2:29-3:10

Please read the passage for the day in at least two different translations, a more formal translation, such as the NRSV, CEB, RSV, or NIV, and then read it again in a freer version or paraphrase such as *The Message*, *Phillip's*, or the *New Living Translation*. As you read, pay attention to images that warrant further exploration:

## LESSON:

### Everyone Who Does Right . . . born of him (1 John 2:29-3:3)

The passage before us, which begins with the last verse of chapter 2, sets up the discussion that follows. It also connects what follows with what went before. In verse 28 of chapter 2 John encourages his readers, who are dealing with the threat of division in their ranks, to abide in him. The word abide appears frequently in Johannine literature. In his farewell address, Jesus tells the disciples to abide in him, as he abides in them, even as the branches abide in the vine. Jesus tells the disciples that they won't bear fruit, unless they abide in the vine (John 15:1-5).

Although John doesn't use the imagery of the "body of Christ," as does Paul, the point is similar—Christian identity is connected to one's relationship with Christ. Here in verse 29 of chapter 2, the author of our letter turns to a strong Johannine image, that of birth. If one knows that God is righteous, and does what is right, then one is born of God. For the modern reader, there is a clear echo to John 3, and Jesus' word to Nicodemus, that he would need to be born from above if he is to enter the realm of God. Here our letter writer, connects being born of God with doing what is right or just. The Greek word translated as righteous in the NRSV is *dikaios*. Too often we read the word "righteous" as "self-righteous," so perhaps a better translation is to read the phrase this way: "if you know that he is just, you may be sure that everyone who does right has been born of him." Raymond Brown suggests that if the word just "is applied to Christ who will return in judgment, not as an enemy but as a friend who gives confidence because he is forgiving," then those who do what is right and are born of God, can have confidence in God's forgiveness, and therefore bear the appropriate fruit.[21]

With this as the lead declaration, John proceeds with the statement that due to God's love, "we should be called children of God" (1 John 3:1). The beginning of Eugene Peterson's translation of verse 1 declares: "What marvelous love the Father has extended to us! Just look at it—we're called children of God!" (*The Message*). Yes, "what marvelous love" has been extended to us. Unfortunately, the world failed to recognize the community's status as children of God because the world knows neither God nor Jesus.

---

21  Raymond E. Brown, *The Epistles of John (Anchor Bible)*, (Garden City, NY: Doubleday, 1982), p. 382.

Since John's community is composed of the children of God—those begotten of God (a reference to being born again?)—they will we be like him. That is, they will be like Christ when he is revealed. What that will be like, is not yet known. In other words, speculation as to the form the children will take when Jesus comes for them, is unwarranted. What is known, is that whatever form he takes, that will be the form the children take. If one has this hope, revealed in this way, they will purify themselves, even as he is pure. In other words, they will purify themselves of sin, a concept well understood in the ancient world, especially within Judaism. In this case, it definitely has an ethical component. That is, if one is a child of God, one will do what is right.

How will we know what is right? In the Johannine scheme of things, one would look to Jesus. As Jesus declared in his Farewell Address, if you've seen Jesus, you've seen the Father (John 14:8-14). If, as we presume here, John's community knew Gospel of John (though it's unlikely they knew the Synoptic Gospels), they would have at least some sense of what this involved. Since we have access to the Synoptics Gospels, we might want to broaden out what it means to be like Jesus.

## The Lawlessness of Sin and the Way of Christ (1 John 3:4-6)

In the previous session, we discovered that the sin John was most concerned about involved schism or separation from the community. Since John's community was formed when members abided in Christ, and therefore in each other, to break the bonds of fellowship (*koinonia*) was to separate one's self from Christ, and therefore enter into sin. John has declared that those who put their hope in God, will purify themselves. That is, they will purge themselves of pollution or sin, which would seem to involve setting aside the impulse to separate from the community. Moving forward John will further define sin as "lawlessness." Thus, if we sin, we are lawless. That leads to the question of what it means to be lawless.

Eugene Peterson offers an intriguing interpretation of this declaration, suggesting in his translation of verse 4 that "sin is a major disruption of God's order" (*The Message*). The Greek word translated as lawlessness is *anomia*, which can also be translated as iniquity or transgression of the law, which is how it is used in the Septuagint version of the Old Testament. All of this suggests that the adversaries of John were advocating a lawless, disordered, licentious lifestyle, and thus they were disrupting God's order. As we move further into the chapter, we discover that John is concerned about the nature of one's allegiance. One is either a child of God or a child of the devil (*ho diabolos*), for if one commits sin, one is a "child of the devil" (1 John 3:8).

Perhaps, we might be stretching the analogy somewhat, but the final episode of Seinfeld illustrates the idea of lawlessness that can take hold of human beings. In this episode, the always self-involved foursome is put on trial for the crime of "depraved indifference." They had been arrested because they stood and watched while an obese man was being robbed. In fact, they didn't just watch, they laughed, cracked jokes, and took pictures. They didn't step into help, because that's who they were. As the trial unfolds, we watch witness after witness, all the wonderful characters who inhabited the show, share how these four people lived with total indifference to the needs and feelings of others. They were, to put it delicately, self-absorbed, or perhaps better—lawless.

With this said, we return to the declaration that in Christ there is no sin, no lawlessness, no iniquity, therefore, those who abide in him, will not sin. As we have already noted, this is a difficult concept to take in. In part this has to do with our definition of sin. If we use the definition of "missing the mark," then it's a matter of aiming high, but not quite getting there. In 1 John sin is defined much more as willful disobedience. Here we're told, that if we abide in Christ, who does not sin, then neither will we sin. As this declaration is made, we're also reminded that Christ came into the world to take away sin. As we've already discovered, Christ came into the world to serve as our advocate/intercessor and as the expiation (atoning sacrifice) for our sins, and for the sins of the world (1 John 2:1-2). In other words, sin is a problem that Jesus came into the world to deal with. One does not know Christ or abide in him if one continues in lawlessness.

As we read this passage, it is important to recognize our tendency to fall short of God's best. We often make choices that run contrary to what is ethical or moral. Having the promise that if we confess our sins, God is faithful to forgive is a word of grace that sustains the journey. What is being envisioned here is not that we fall short, but that we intentionally act in ways that are inappropriate, and that this is an expression of lawlessness. William Self writes in his homiletical advice to preachers of this text, that the false teachers whom John faces, appear to be taking a gnostic view of things, in which body and spirit are seen as separate from each other, therefore, the adversaries seem to be suggesting that "satisfying all the lusts of the body was acceptable. The gnostic said that spiritual people can indulge in sin and not be harmed."[22] John disagrees wholeheartedly with this vision.

## Don't Be Deceived—the Righteous Do Right (1 John 3:7-10)

Once again, John addresses his community as "little children" (Greek *teknion*). This has become a regular address, suggesting a paternal relationship existing between John and the community. Acting in paternal fashion, John warns the community to avoid being deceived. John doesn't identify the nature of this deception. It could be the Christological issue that emerged in chapter 2, in which questions were raised as to whether Jesus was the Christ (1 John 2:22). It could also relate to whether one could abide in Christ and indulge the flesh (sin). Whatever the nature of this deception, John insists that if you're righteous (act justly), you will do what is

---

22  William I. Self, "Third Sunday of Easter: Homiletical Perspective," in *Feasting on the Word. Year B, Volume 2: Lent Through Eastertide,* David L. Bartlett and Barbara Brown Taylor, eds., (Louisville: Westminster John Knox Press, 2008), p. 423.

right (just). To act righteously is to follow the example of Jesus. As Raymond Brown points out, this is the third time Jesus is said to be just/righteous (2:1, 29), making it "part of the author's campaign to put emphasis on the way Jesus lived and died."[23]

If those who abide in Christ are children of God, what can be said about those who fail to abide in Christ? We ought to keep in mind that our author has a strongly dualistic view of reality. Thus, for John, if a person isn't a child of God, then that person is a child of the devil. The test of one's parentage is seen in the way one acts. To act acts sinfully is a sign that one is a child of the devil.

It is worth noting that this is the first use of the word *dia-bolos* or devil in 1 John, though John has previously spoken of the Evil One. All the uses of the word devil are found in verse 8 (three uses) and verse 10 (one use). To make this contrast complete, John declares that the devil has been sinning from the beginning. The words "the beginning" play a significant role in the Johannine literature. John opens the letter revealing that what follows goes back to the beginning. In this case, the beginning of the Christian movement (1 John 1:1). In the Gospel of John, we hear the declaration that "in the beginning was the Word" (John 1:1). Now, we hear that the devil has been sinning since the beginning. In essence, John is saying that sinning is the reason the devil exists. Raymond Brown writes that "from the devil's appearance on the scene at the beginning of human history, he has been active, and the author is worried that now the devil is active in 'the last hour.'"[24] If, the devil has been engaged in sinning (rebelling) from the beginning, John notes that Christ came into the world "to destroy the works of the devil" (vs. 8).

References to the devil are problematic for modern progressive Christians. I know that I struggle with the idea, especially if the devil is understood to be a personalized power who poses a threat to God. Much of this is due to our discomfort with supernatural-ism, the idea that oppositional spiritual forces are intervening in

---

23  Brown, *Epistles of John,* p. 404.
24  Brown, *Epistles of John,* p. 406.

our world. Yet, it's clear from reading the Gospels that Jesus was an exorcist. He was known as one who cast out demons. Richard Beck points our attention to Peter's proclamation of the Gospel to Cornelius, in which Peter tells Cornelius that Jesus "went around doing good and healing all who were under the power of the devil, because God was with him. (Acts 10:37-38) Beck notes that while many modern Christians love the Jesus who goes around doing good, the "holy rebel facing down oppressive social, political, and religious institutions," like "Thomas Jefferson, we ignore the second part, which deals with Jesus overcoming the "power of the devil." Beck writes: "And yet, over and over in the New Testament, Jesus' witness and example—his good works—are consistently described as *spiritual warfare,* as a battle he was waging with Satan." Beck follows this up by pointing our attention to the summary of Jesus' work in the world found in 1 John 3:8: "The reason the Son of God appeared was to destroy the devil's work (NIV)."[25] In other words, if we're to make sense of Jesus and his ministry we must take into consideration how he saw his own ministry, as well as how early Christians understood that ministry. We might be uncomfortable with this world view, but it is part of the biblical story. If we want to take Jesus seriously, we must face up to the full gospel story.

Having warned the readers about taking the devil seriously, John points us back to Jesus. He has come to destroy the devil's work. John's message is that a person's actions reflect a person's parentage (we are the fruit of the tree to which we belong). Having identified the parentage of those who act contrary to God's ways, and the fruit of that parentage, in verse 9, John turns to the children of God. He declares that if one is born of God, that person will not sin. However, one defines sin, those who are born of God (born from above/born again) do not sin. The reason the children of God do not sin is that God's seed (Gk. *sperma)* abides in them. As to the nature of this seed, scholars are not of one mind. This has led to dif- fering translations of the verse. Consider for a moment the *Phillips*

---

25    Richard Beck, *Reviving Old Scratch: Demons and the Devil for Doubters and the Disenchanted,* (Minneapolis: Fortress Press, 2016), pp. 30-31.

translation of the verse: "The man who is really God's son does not
practise sin, for *God's nature* is in him, for good, and such a heredity
is incapable of sin." In the mind of J.B. Phillips, the *sperma* is God's
nature, which indwells the believer.   Whatever the exact meaning
of the word, the point seems to be clear. The *Common English Bible*
takes a rather modern stab at the word, trying to communicate its
essence, declaring that "those born from God don't practice sin
because *God's DNA* remains in them." The footnote offers this a
clarification of the use of DNA, offering "genetic character." Again,
that is a modern rendition, but it gets us close to John's meaning.
As Clifton Black points out the language is metaphorical and not
scientific, but it does convey a key point regarding being born of
God, they "have within them by God's insemination as it were, the
permanent evidence of their recognizable character as children of
God." He goes on to put this in more modern, but metaphorical
terms: "Righteous conduct is the genetic imprint that distinguishes
a child of God (3:10; cf. 3:1; John 1:12-13)."[26]

In verse 10, John restates the issue by laying out the contrast
between the children of God and the children of the devil. As for
the latter, "all who do not do what is right are not from God, nor
are those who do not love their brothers and sisters." Note here the
reference to loving brothers and sisters. In this letter, the brothers
and sisters are members of the community. Those who are children
of the devil have demonstrated their allegiance by the way they have
treated members of the community. Going back to chapter 2, this
would include the act of dividing the community (schism). Who
we are is revealed by our behavior. While John understands that not
everyone has reached perfection, which is why we have an advocate
(*paraclete*) (1 John 2:1), the expectation is that we will move toward
that perfect state. Using the light/darkness metaphor, we will be
moving closer and closer to the light, who is God.

---

26   C. Clifton Black, "The First, Second, and Third Letters of John," in *New
Interpreter's Bible,* Leander Keck, ed., (Nashville: Abingdon Press, 1998),
12:414.

## QUESTIONS FOR MEDITATION AND DISCUSSION:

1.   1 John 2:28, provides the link between the earlier conversation in chapter 2 the verse we ended the previous session with declares: "And now, little children, abide in him, so that when he is revealed we may have confidence and not be put to shame before him at his coming." How is it that by abiding in God through Christ, we may have the confidence we need so that we might "not be put to shame at his coming?" How does this confidence relate to our ability to do what is right, as is expected of one who is born of God?

2.   What does the declaration that "we are children of God" suggest to you? What does it mean to be a child of God? What does that have to do with doing what is right or just?

3.   John writes that the one who sins is lawless. What does the use of the word "lawless" suggest? Eugene Peterson's translation of verse 4, suggests that under this view, sin is a "major disruption of God's order." With this translation in mind, what is sin?

4.   In verse 7, John comes back to his concern about the danger of deception. What is the concern here? What kind of deception might he have in mind?

5.   Keeping in mind John's dualistic theology, in which light and darkness are regularly contrasted, noting that he has already spoken of his community in terms of being "children of God," what do you make of him speaking of his opponents as "children of the devil?"

   A. Remembering that John speaks of the devil three times in verse 8 (and once in verse 10), what is the mark of being a child of the devil?

   B. Since the word "beginning" is important to the Johannine message, how might we understand the reference to the devil sinning from the beginning? Raymond

Brown suggests that the meaning here is that sinning is the devil's reason for existing, and therefore has been fulfilling that purpose ever since the beginning; what do you make of this?

C. How do you feel about the reference to the devil? Why are modern Christians often uncomfortable with the idea of the devil? Following Richard Beck, if we remove references to the devil, how will we understand Jesus' ministry, which in 1 John involves destroying the work of the devil, and in the Gospels engaging in what is often called exorcism?

6.  In verse 9, John returns to the children of God, declaring that they cannot sin, for they have within them the seed of God. Clifton Black suggests that John seems to be saying that those who are born of God, have within them the permanent evidence of their character as children of God. We might speak of this as an indelible mark placed on them, which enables them to not sin (engage in lawlessness). If this is true, how does it inform both our understanding of sin, and the expectations placed on the children of God? How is behavior a mark of one's abiding with God?

7.  In the last verse in this section, we're told that not only is sin a mark of those who are the children of the devil, but the same is true of their lack of love for their brothers and sisters in the community. If we go back to the top to 1 John 2:28, how might we understand the intent of this conversation as a preparation for the coming of Christ? How does our behavior demonstrate our readiness to welcome Jesus?

EXERCISE:

One of the major questions that arises in 1 John is the identity of the opponents. It is clear that one group has seceded, and that scholars detect the possibility that the seceders had gnostic tendencies. The stress on behavior being the mark of the continued presence of sin, suggests that the secessionists have argued in an early gnostic way that behavior doesn't matter. They are not under any form of law, which leads to what has been called antinomianism. Doing an internet search, look up antinomian groups. What is the antinomian argument? Why might one adopt it? Do you see any similarities between these groups and what the author of 1 John suggests about his opponents?

## A CALL TO PRAYER:

*O God, may our lives demonstrate that we are your children. May we move toward that experience of your presence so that sin no longer dominates our identity. Amen.*

# SESSION 5

## LOVE ONE ANOTHER
### 1 John 3:11-24

## VISION:

What is love and how is it expressed? That is the question we take up as we explore the remainder of 1 John 3. We are to love one another, not only in word, but also in deed. If we obey God's commandments that express that love, then we will abide in God, and God will abide in us.

## READING: 1 JOHN 3:11-24

Please read the passage for the day in at least two different translations, a more formal translation, such as the NRSV, CEB, RSV, or NIV, and then read it again in a freer version or paraphrase such as *The Message*, *Phillip's*, or the *New Living Translation*. As you read, pay attention to images that warrant further exploration.

## LESSON:

### Love One another as Christ Loves (1 John 3:11-17)

The first lines of the letter "declare what was from the beginning." What was declared from the beginning concerned the word of life, the foundation of the fellowship the believers had with one another (1 John 1:1-4). In 1 John 3:11, John once again speaks of the message heard from the beginning. That message was that they should love one another. Raymond Brown suggests that this reference to "the beginning" could mark the beginning of a new section, part two, of the essay. He notes that the phrase "this is the gospel"—his translation—appears only here in verse 11 and in 1 John 1:5 in the letter. The message that is proclaimed in the second part of the letter is more focused on the need for love to be experienced within the community than the hostility that comes from outside.[27]

Even if John focuses more on the situation existing within the community, he doesn't forget the threat from outside. He remains concerned about those who have disturbed the fellowship due to their alliance with the evil one (the devil) that led to schism. We see this in the reference to Cain, who stands as an example of one who made alliance with the evil one. This alliance led to fratricide. The reason Cain acted as he did, was that his deeds were evil, while his brother's actions were righteous. While Scripture doesn't ever reveal the reason why God rejected Cain's offering and deemed his brother's offering as being righteous, in John's view, the fact that Cain killed his brother was a clear example, as D. Moody Smith notes, of "the consequence of failing to heed the love commandment. The opposite of love for one's brother is hatred leading to murder (vs. 15)."[28] Here again, we see the dualistic vision that permeates the letter.

In his attempt to encourage this fledgling community, John reminds its members that they should expect hostility from outside the community. After all, the world hates them, because of their love for one another. Continuing the binary vision, he suggests that love is an expression of life, and hate is an expression of death. Those who hate are murderers, just like Cain. Beyond this, murderers do not have eternal life in them. As we ponder this word, it is good to remember that in John's view, one's deeds are rooted in

---

27   Raymond Brown, *Epistles of John (Anchor Bible)*, (Garden City, NY: Doubleday and Co., 1982), 467.

28   D. Moody Smith, *First, Second, and Third John (Interpretation: A Bible Commentary for Teaching and Preaching)*, (Louisville: John Knox Press, 1991), p. 88.

one's orientation—to God or to the devil. While mention is made of the world hating members of the John's community, contextually those who hate are the secessionists. Remember that Cain kills his brother, not someone outside the family.

It is here that John brings in the example of Jesus. We know love, because we have the example of Jesus, who laid his life down for us. We ought to do the same. When it comes to the biblical idea of love, I can't think of a better pop culture example than the closing scenes of the old Star Trek movie: *The Wrath of Kahn*. In this film, Captain Kirk's old nemesis, Kahn, tries to destroy the Enterprise. The crew has only one hope of survival. Spock must fix the warp drive to keep the ship from exploding. To do this Spock must enter a radiation-filled reactor room and cap the reactor. Spock goes into the room and fixes the problem, knowing that he won't come out alive. His crew mates are saved and appreciative, but they regret their loss. However, Spock has the last word. Trapped by his own choice in the reactor room, he tells Jim Kirk that "the needs of the many outweigh the needs of the few, or the one." Although Spock is a person of logic and never shows emotion, I would suggest that his action was truly an act of love for his crew mates. By laying down his life for his friends, Jesus shows us the fullness of God's love, and encourages us to do the same.

The question is: how do we follow this pathway? John isn't asking us to die. He's asking us to live sacrificially for others. This means living a life of service to humanity with the hope that the world might be transformed. In his willingness to give his life as an expression of God's love for the world, Jesus gives us a hint as to the true nature of the Christian faith. It's really not about me. It's about the Other. John asks: How does God's love abide in one who "has the world's goods and sees a brother or sister in need and yet refuses to help?" (vs. 17). This directive, in context, refers to members of the community (brothers and sisters), not necessarily those outside the community. A good example of this is found in the book of Acts, where it is said that the people shared all things in common, and thus no one was in need (Acts 4:32). The question then concerns how we might expand beyond the immediate community. That is, for Christians experiencing affluence, can this word concerning caring for the community need to be universalized? But, even as we do this, we might ask the prior question of our responsibility for members of the community?

## Love in Deed, Not Word (1 John 3:18-22)

Having asked how one could say one was a loving person, while refusing one's brother or sister in need in verse 17, John reinforces his message by telling the community: "let us love, not in word or speech, but in truth and action" (vs. 18). The opening verse of this section builds off the statement in verse 17. How can you say you love God and not help a brother or sister in need? Thus, love is a verb. It requires action, which will lead to reassured hearts. Again, we are confronted with the question of whether John intends for this instruction to apply only within the community or whether it can be applied beyond it.

Ever present in John's mind is the challenge posed by the secessionists. The secessionists have been suggesting that faith alone is necessary for salvation, without any corresponding deeds. The issue, as Raymond Brown notes, isn't hypocrisy. The issue is the secessionists "taught that actions or deeds were not salvifically important since one already possessed eternal life though faith in Christ."[29] In this we see a strong resemblance between John's message and that of James, who declared that "faith by itself, if it has no works, is dead" (James 2:14-17). As we have seen, John does have a place for grace— "if anyone sins, we have an advocate with the Father, Jesus Christ the Righteous" (1 John 2:1-2), but grace doesn't let a person off the hook. Love, like faith, requires action.

It is action that provides reassurance that one is from the truth. Action is related to conscience. But if our hearts do condemn us, God is greater still, and thus there is hope. As Eugene Peterson puts it in his translation: "For God is greater than our worried hearts and knows more about us than we do ourselves. (vs. 20).

---

29  Brown, *Epistles of John*, p. 476.

Therefore, if once our hearts are no longer condemning us, then we will have boldness before God. There remains the commitment to the perfection of faith as a goal. The secessionists, however, emphasizing faith over deeds, may have offered an attractive pathway. Raymond Brown offers this interpretation: "One is begotten by God through faith in Jesus, and deeds cannot change that. But the author refuses to concede that the need of showing the truth of love in deeds must lead to a lack of confidence about one's status before God."[30] Concern for action does not negate God's forgiveness or acceptance. That might be the point. They couldn't be bold in their proclamation of the Gospel, because they lacked the confidence rooted in the love of God.

The question of boldness before God climaxes in verse 22, with the promise that "we receive whatever we ask from him because we keep his commandments and do what pleases him" (CEB). The idea here is that a covenantal relationship with God involves keeping God's commandments. By being in tune with God's will, one likely will have one's prayers answered. It is, therefore, a reciprocal relationship that is evidenced by one's actions.

## Abiding in Christ through the Spirit (1 John 3:23-24)

In the concluding two verses of chapter 3, we find a summation of the previous point concerning the commandments of God. John identifies the commandment of God in this way: "we should believe in the name of his Son Jesus Christ and love one another" (vs. 23). There are two commandments to be followed. First, members of the community should believe in Jesus and love each other. The word "believe" has become problematic in recent years, in large part due to theological reductionism that reduced belief to affirming doctrinal statements. If you believe the formula set out in the doctrinal statement, then you will be saved. That perspective sounds more like the secessionists than John. Believing here is more than agreeing to doctrinal statements. We should note that John

---

30  Brown, *Epistles of John,* p. 478.

uses the singular—commandment—so that to believe involves loving one another. This word stands close to the Synoptic tradition
of the two commandments—love God and love one's neighbor
(Mark 12:28-31). Judith Lieu confirms my thinking, noting that
for John, belief in Jesus and loving one another belong together.
Thus, "the vertical dimension of belief and the horizontal dimension of reciprocal love are inseparable: "we" and "one another" are
those who so believe."[31]

As the chapter closes, we encounter the common Johannine
word *abide*. Those who obey God's commands abide in God and
God abides in them. It is not a matter of meriting God's favor. It
is simply a matter of a covenant relationship. To abide is to obey,
and when one abides in God, God abides in them. We know that
God abides in us through the presence of the Spirit within us.
As Raymond Brown puts it: "The same God who *gave* the commandment (3:23c) *gave* the Spirit that enables us to live out the
commandment."[32]

The reference here to the Spirit, at the end of chapter 3, connects what has gone before with what is to come. In 1 John 4:1-6
speaks of testing the spirits. Even as there is the Holy Spirit, there
are other spirits who are not of God. By obeying God's commandments, one gives evidence that God's Spirit is present. This vision
of the Spirit fits well with Gospel of John's vision of the Spirit as the
Paraclete, the Comforter/Counselor/Advocate, who bears witness
to God's truth.

## QUESTIONS FOR MEDITATION AND DISCUSSION:

1.  When we come to 1 John 3:11, we appear to be at a turning
    point in the letter. John reaffirms the gospel/message heard

---

31  Judith M. Lieu. *I, II, & III John: A Commentary (New Testament Library)*,
    (Louisville: Westminster John Knox Press, 2008), (Kindle Locations
    2771-2772).
32  Brown, *Epistles of John*, p. 482.

from the beginning. How is this message of love the foundation of the Gospel?

2. John refers to the Old Testament figure of Cain. How does John use Cain in presenting his understanding of the Gospel? How does this story encapsulate John's dualistic theology?

3. In verses 14-16, John's dualism is presented in terms of two trajectories—hate and love—how do these two poles express themselves, in John's understanding? What do you make of how John lays out this vision?

4. The principle of love gets put into practice in verse 17. What is the example of how love is expressed? Is this a command that applies only within the community? Compare this call to love in the Johannine community to the description in Acts 4:32 of the Jerusalem Community—do you see similarities or differences? Can this be universalized?

5. What is the difference between loving in word or speech and loving in truth and action? Why is the former insufficient?

6. When it comes to love in truth and action, how might our hearts reassure us that we are from the truth? How does a loving heart lead to boldness before God? (vs. 19-21)

7. John suggests that if we obey the commandments of God we will receive whatever we ask. How might you interpret this statement and put it into practice? (vs. 22) How might this be misinterpreted and misapplied? How do we guard against this?

8. As we come to the close of the chapter, how do you read John's statement concerning the commandment (note the singular) to believe in the name of Jesus and love one another.

   A. How might these two seemingly different commands be one commandment? How are they related?

B. How might this command relate to Jesus' two great
    commandments—love of God and love of neighbor
    (Mark 12:28-31)?

9.   In the concluding word, how do you read the relationship
     between obeying God's commandments and abiding in God?
     How does the Spirit witness to our abiding in God?

## EXERCISE:

John makes note of the Old Testament figure of Cain. He is
portrayed here as one who is aligned with the Evil One, and thus
an example of those who are unrighteous. Using a Bible Dictionary or Commentary, explore the story of Cain (Genesis 4:1-26).
Compare how John uses the story of Cain to the way the author
of Genesis portrays him.  Is Cain portrayed as an evil person, or
someone who commits an evil act?

## A CALL TO PRAYER:

*Gracious One, may we abide in you so that we might demonstrate
in and through our lives that we love you and one another, as you have
commanded us. Amen*

# SESSION 6

## TESTING THE SPIRITS

### 1 John 4:1-6

## VISION:

We live in a disenchanted world. It is a feature of the world existing after the dawn of the Enlightenment. To be modern is to assume that one can only believe what is tangible. John writes in a different era, an enchanted era when God was understood to be active in the world. In that context, John speaks of two spirits at work in the world. There is the Spirit of truth and the spirit of error. We should embrace the first and reject the second. The quest for discernment is rooted in Christology. As we'll see, there is good news. That news is that one can conquer the World through Christ.

## READING: 1 JOHN 4:1-6

Please read the passage for the day in at least two different translations, a more formal translation, such as the NRSV, CEB, RSV, or NIV, and then read it again in a freer version or paraphrase such as *The Message*, *Phillip's*, or the *New Living Translation*. As you read, pay attention to images that warrant further exploration.

## LESSON:

### Confession is Good for the Soul—1 John 4:1-3

In the previous lesson, we read about God's commandment concerning belief in Christ Jesus and loving one another. Those who obey this commandment—note that this is one commandment, not two—abide in Christ, and Christ abides in them. We know this to be true because of the witness of the Spirit given to us by God. It is the Spirit who bears witness to Christ. This is the Spirit (Paraclete) that Jesus promised to send to the disciples, telling them that the Spirit will "teach you everything, and remind you of all that I have said to you" (John 14:25-26). Although the Spirit bears witness to Christ, allowing us to abide in Christ, we must be aware that not every spirit is from God. Believers must test the spirits. Once again, we're reminded that the survival of the community is threatened by adversaries to the truth. Therefore, the community needs to be wary of those who come to them saying that they come from God. In these six verses of 1 John 4, the author instructs the community on how the can discern the difference between the Spirit of truth and the spirit of error.

As we approach this passage it is good to keep in mind that most Western Christians live in a disenchanted world. We may speak of the Spirit, but we're not necessarily given over to the idea that a spiritual world exists like the one described in the biblical text. At one level, it is right and good to pursue scientific answers to life's questions. It's good to integrate the answers we receive from science into our faith. The more we pursue scientific answers the more we move into doubt and disenchantment. But, as Richard Beck suggests, we are "skeptical and scientific people, yes, but we're also haunted by the suspicion that the universe is more than the sum of its subatomic parts."[33] With that in mind, perhaps we can approach this passage with an openness to learn from a voice that embraces a more enchanted world view.

Reading 1 John is difficult for those who have embraced a disenchanted view of the world. Perhaps that is why we focus on the command to love one another and leave aside the words about a spiritual realm. However, the call to love doesn't make sense unless it's read in the broader context of the spiritual battle being waged by the believers. It's possible, of course, to make the "mys-

33   Richard Beck, *Reviving Old Scratch: Demons and the Devil for Doubters and the Disenchanted. (Theology for the People)*, (Minneapolis: Fortress Press, 2016), p. 16.

tery" present in the text a little less bold. We see this played out somewhat in Eugene Peterson's translation of the passage. Take the opening line of the chapter. While the NRSV opens with *"Beloved, do not believe every spirit, . . .,"* the Peterson translation reads: *"My dear friends, don't believe everything you hear."* It might seem like a minor difference, but Peterson's translation seems designed to be more palatable for Western Christians who are uncomfortable with mystery. Of course, we shouldn't believe everything we hear. Fake news is plentiful, especially in the realm of social media. Nonetheless, I don't think this is what John has in mind. He's concerned not only about lying preachers, but false prophets who claim to have inside knowledge of the things of God that might lead the community astray.

To get at the root of the matter, John wants us to discern what lies underneath a person's actions. For John, there are two kinds of spirits—good and evil. Raymond Brown notes that these two spirits manifest themselves in human behavior and are seen in either true of false confessions of faith. He writes: "A true confession comes from the Spirit of God, an erroneous confession indicates not only the absence of the Spirit of God, but also the presence of the wicked Spirit of Deceit (4:6e)."[34]

Why is John concerned about these spirits? What does he fear might happen? From the broader context, John is concerned that the adversaries, the ones who had left the community over a doctrinal dispute, were intent on making converts from among those who remained within the community. If this community has suffered schism, it is understandable that there would be attempts to poach those who remained. We see this happen regularly in church splits. The side that leaves often tries to sow discord, in the hope of drawing to their side those who are conflicted. That seems to be the case here. John wants to make sure that those who remained faithful are not tempted by the designs of the opponents. That is

---

34   Raymond Brown, *Epistles of John (Anchor Bible)*, (Garden City, NY: Doubleday and Co., 1982), p. 486.

because the opponents are the anti-Christ, a word that appears once again in this chapter.

The question is, how do you know if a prophet has the Spirit of God? What is the test that enables you to discern the difference between truth and error? John goes straight to the point. As he did before (1 John 2:22), the test is the confession that Jesus Christ came in the flesh. Those who speak truth are moved by the Spirit of God, and they will affirm the incarnation. Prophets don't speak of their own accord, they are led by the spirit speaking through them. This principle is laid out in 2 Peter, which declares: *"First of all you must understand this, that no prophecy of scripture is a matter of one's own interpretation, because no prophecy ever came by human will, but men and women moved by the Holy Spirit spoke from God"* (2 Peter 1:20-21). The problem facing the community is that many false prophets have gone out into the world, and they have been moved by the spirit of deceit. The nature of this deceit is negating the importance of Jesus, and this is the spirit of the anti-Christ. As Raymond Brown puts it, "the author is identifying the secessionists collectively with the predicted false prophets of the last times who 'will deceive many' (Matthew 24:11)."[35]

The matter that led to the division within John's community was Christological. Those who seceded left the community and aligned themselves with the world. So, the matter of the false prophets is rather specific. It's not just "lying preachers" in general, but those who embraced a false Christology that negated Jesus. He is speaking to his community, warning them not to be taken in by the false prophets' theological vision. Thus, the issue here is different from the one that Paul was dealing with in 1 Corinthians. That was a question about whether all the *charisms* came from the one Spirit. Here the question is whether the words of certain prophets come from the Evil One. All of this is to be understood in an eschatological context, in which John and his community expected the spirit of Antichrist to be revealed.

---

35  Brown, *Epistles of John*, pp. 489-490.

This leads to the question of the nature of the confession. If, as it appears to be true, the opponents once had been part of the Johannine community and then chose to leave, they are like family that has been broken apart. They had been baptized with the same baptism. They also had received the gift of the Holy Spirit. Unfortunately, at some point in time there was a fissure in the community, and the two parties took different paths. In John's view this fissure came about because the secessionists had embraced a different spirit from the one they encountered in Jesus. In other words, they had chosen to embrace heresy. For many progressive Christians, the word "heresy" is problematic. Many contrast orthopraxis (right action) with orthodoxy (right belief), placing an emphasis on orthopraxis. For John, orthopraxis and orthodoxy are one and the same. How one views Jesus is a clue to one's relationship with God, and the way one acts. If one is to abide in God, then one must abide in Jesus, who came in the flesh (incarnation), and who in that incarnation brought salvation to humanity. If one abides in Christ, then one will act accordingly. Apparently, the secessionists have a different understanding of Jesus and his work.

What we don't know is whether the secessionists had a fully developed docetic Christology, one that denied Jesus' physicality. We know that Docetism was being propagated early in the second century, as evidenced by the writings of figures like Ignatius of Antioch, but we don't know how far back this heterodox teaching goes. Raymond Brown isn't convinced that the secessionists were docetists in the same manner as Ignatius' opponents. He believes that "the issue is not that the secessionists are denying the incarnation or the physical reality of Jesus' humanity; they are denying that what Jesus was or did in the flesh was related to his being the Christ, i.e. was salvific."[36] Other interpreters do see a more docetic Christology present, but in either case the opponents have denied the value of Jesus' physical being to his salvific work. This hyper-spirituality can have negative effects on one's engagement in this world. So, even if this isn't a fully developed docetic vision,

---

36   Brown, *Epistles of John,* p. 505.

there is a movement in that direction, at the very least. Jaime Clark-Soles makes this notation:

> Knowing is doing, and knowing rightly is tied to acting rightly. Those who disembody Jesus easily disembody their neighbor. Certain ways of "knowing" cause arrogance and disdain of others in the community.[37]

In John's mind, theology matters. How you envision Jesus and his work matters. It matters in relationship to one's behavior. In what he perceived to be the "last times," behavior was important.

## Conquering the World (1 John 4:4-6)

Having called on the community to test the spirits of those claiming to speak for God and have laid out a Christological criterion for that test, John moves on to commend his community. He wants to encourage them. He uses one of his favorite phrases—"little children." While the phrase has a paternalistic air to it, that is not uncommon in the New Testament. Speaking to the "little children," the founders of the community want to make sure it stays true to its founding purpose. Since they stayed true to their founding purpose, they receive a word of affirmation: "You are from God, and have conquered them," (vs. 4a) that is the false spirits. To put this in modern terms, they had resisted the representatives of the Antichrist, who tried to scam them by posing as prophets proclaiming divine truth. They saw through the scam and hung up the phone (or deleted the email).

Why were they able to do this? According to John it is because *"the one who is in you is greater than the one who is in the world"* (vs 4b). Once again John expresses himself in dualistic terms, contrasting the one identified by Jesus as the Spirit of Truth (John 14:16-17) with the spirit inhabiting the world—the spirit of the

---

37  Jaime Clark-Soles, "First, Second, and Third John," in *Fortress Commentary on the Bible: Two Volume Set*, Gale A. Yee, ed., (Minneapolis: Fortress Press, 2014), (Kindle Locations 56833-56834). Kindle Edition.

Antichrist. Earlier in the letter John wrote to the community, commending the young people, because they had *"conquered the Evil One"* (1 John 2:13-14). Now, as Raymond Brown notes, John tells the reader that conquering the Evil One is due to the presence of the Spirit, who is stronger than the Evil One, and that "this victory had been won in terms of a victory over the secessionists."[38]

When we move into verse 5, John addresses these very secessionists, whom the remnant had faithfully resisted. He writes that the opponents are from the world, and therefore what they have to say is derived from that world, even as the world listens to them. For John, to be in the world is the opposite of being in God. By world, John doesn't mean the physical world, but rather the spirit of this world, the spirit that resists God. Theologian H. Richard Niebuhr, in his classic *Christ and Culture*, characterized John's vision as being an expression of the "Christ against Culture" paradigm. There is, in John's vision a complete rejection of the broader culture, a separation between the children of God and the children of this world.

That world appears as a realm under the power of evil; it is the region of darkness, into which the citizens of the kingdom of light must not enter; it is characterized by the prevalence in it of lies, hatred, and murder; it is the heir of Cain. It is a secular society, dominated by the *"lust of the flesh, the lust of the eyes and the pride of life,"* or, in Prof. Dodd's translation of these phrases it is *"pagan society, with its sensuality, superficiality and pretentiousness, it's materialism and its egoism."* It is a culture that is concerned with temporal and passing values, whereas Christ has words of eternal life; it is a dying as well as a murderous order, for "the world passes away and the lust of it."[39]

Set against the world with its temporal and passing values is the Johannine Community, which is from God, and therefore is marked by the promise of eternal life. John writes to the communi-

---

38  Brown, *Epistles of John,* p. 498.
39  H. Richard Niebuhr, *Christ and Culture,* (New York: Harper Torch Books, 1951), p. 48.

ty, noting that they were from God, and that those who were from God listened to them. Those who are not of God (from the world) don't listen to them. So, *"from this we know the spirit of truth and the spirit of error"* ("spirit of falsehood" NIV).

If the author of 1 John embraced *"Christ against Culture"* vision, is this a vision that is appropriate for the contemporary church. For John, the broader culture was pagan in orientation and he lived under a Roman imperial system. For Christians living in the West, the world has become increasingly secular, and yet for the most part Christianity remains the dominant religious force, at least as an organized religious force. John's vision is sectarian in nature, but those who find themselves in mainstream Protestant, Catholic, and Orthodox churches are anything but sectarian. In fact, both conservative and liberal Christians in the United States tend to orient themselves toward particular political and social entities. Thus, as Clifton Black suggests, John's sectarian vision *"would hardly endear this literature to Christians along the twenty-first century main-line, among those inclined to engage, if not to embrace, the world beyond the church."*[40]

John writes to a church living under threat from external forces that he defines in spiritual terms. He also writes with an eschatological vision that suggests the end is near. Living in a much different context, most contemporary Christians will find this vision rather foreign, or if they embrace the message on a surface level, they may miss the point of the letter. So, even if we're put off by John's sectarianism, at the very least the message found here might serve as a helpful warning against drawing so close to the broader culture that the church gets swallowed up, and it loses its prophetic voice.

---

40  C. Clifton Black, "The First, Second, and Third Letters of John," in *New Interpreter's Bible: A Commentary in Twelve Volumes,* (Nashville: Abingdon Press, 1998), 12:428.

## QUESTIONS FOR MEDITATION AND DISCUSSION

1.  It is suggested by many that due to the Enlightenment and the influence of science we live in a disenchanted world. What does a disenchanted world look like? And how does such a world view affect one's faith in God?

2.  At the end of chapter 3 of 1 John, the author writes that the way we know that we abide in God is that the Spirit of God is present. As chapter 4 begins, John tells the Beloved community not to believe every spirit, but to test every spirit. What does this statement about testing the spirits suggest to you about the nature of faith?

3.  How does John suggest we test the spirits? What are the criteria for testing?

4.  What does it mean that the spirit that comes from God confesses that Jesus Christ has come in the flesh? Why would John make this the criterion?

5.  What is the nature of the spirit that fails to confess that Jesus came in the flesh? What is the spirit of the Antichrist mentioned here in verse 3?

6.  In verse four, John commends the community because they are from God, and because they have conquered "them." Who might "them" be? How did they conquer?

7.  John speaks in verse 4 of the one who is in them being greater than the one who is in the world. Who is John speaking of, and why would he speak this way about the world?

8.  In verses 5 and 6, John contrasts those who listen to the world and those who listen to God. What kind of relationship do you think John wants the community to have with the culture? Do you sense here a form of sectarianism, what H. Richard Niebuhr calls "Christ against Culture?"

9.  As we think about the relationship with the world, or the culture, what should our relationship be with the culture? What might the dangers be to the church and to us as God's people if we get too cozy with our culture?

10. From what we read here, do you get the sense that God and the Evil One are in a stalemate, or God has already won the victory? At the same time, do you see a way for this community to engage the broader world?

## EXERCISE:

In his book, *Christ and Culture,* theologian H. Richard Niebuhr suggests that 1 John exemplifies the "Christ against Culture" paradigm. Accessing Niebuhr's book, compare and contrast this paradigm with the four other paradigms: Christ of Culture, Christ above Culture, Christ and Culture in Paradox, and Christ the Transformer of Culture. Which of these paradigms or models do you find the most helpful to you as you consider your relationship to culture?

## A CALL TO PRAYER:

*John might put things in ways that are more black and white than we may be comfortable with, but we pray for a spirit of discernment, so that we might navigate the challenges posed by our culture.*

# SESSION 7

## BEHOLD THE LOVE OF GOD

### 1 John 4:7-21

### VISION:

1 John is best known for its declaration that God is love, and that those who love God will love one another. In this lesson, we come face to face with this message, which is set within a broader, more dualistic message of encouragement to a beleaguered community. The question for this session concerns how we can hear this word in its original context and then bring it more fully into ours.

### READING: 1 JOHN 4:7-21

Please read the passage for the day in at least two different translations, a more formal translation, such as the NRSV, CEB, RSV, or NIV, and then read it again in a freer version or paraphrase such as *The Message, Phillip's,* or the *New Living Translation.* As you read, pay attention to images that warrant further exploration:

### LESSON:

### God is love! (1 John 4:7-12)

In the previous lesson, John wrote to his community, warning them that not every spirit came from God. He told them to test the spirits. The test involved the confession that Jesus came in the flesh. If a person made the confession, then they were from God. If not, then they reject this witness. The opening sections of 1 John reveal the harsh realities facing the early church. At least for a moment, we turn to a more appealing section of the letter.

John makes the declaration that God is love and that those who claim to love God will love one another. This is the other side of the coin. The confession that Jesus came in the flesh is inseparably linked to one's love for one another. Even as the confession that Jesus came in the flesh is foundational to the life of faith, so is love. Everything is built on this two-fold premise. The confession of faith in the God revealed in Jesus is fully embodied. Since God is love, those who embrace God, will love one another. Again, confession of faith and love of others are separable, because God is love. Therefore, you can't say that you are from God and not love.

In 1 John 4 it becomes clear that in addition to ideas such as truth, light, and life, which stand out in the Johannine texts, one can add the word *agapē* or love. Love, like the other qualities mentioned, comes from above. It is an expression of being begotten of God. As Raymond Brown puts it:

> The connection of ideas is this: God is love; the offspring He begets must be marked by love; by loving, the children come to know their Father. This is an application of the general principle that human beings are in the likeness of God, but now that likeness is not through creation but through faith and love.[41]

If God is love, then God's people should express that reality in their own lives. In fact, if love is not present in one's life, then one is not begotten of God. That is, they are not born from above (John 3:3).

What we have here is one of the most explicit and eloquent statements about love to be found in the New Testament. Only the words of 1 Corinthians 13 are better known than these words. As D. Moody Smith notes, this statement is even more definitive than Paul's word. Here we find a "distinctly Christian explanation

---

41   Raymond Brown, *The Epistles of John (Anchor Bible)*, (Garden City, NY: Doubleday and Co., 1982), p. 548.

of the origin and human motivation of love, one that has become a classical model for theology and ethics."[42]

John moves on to explain that the way in which God, who is love, is revealed to humanity, is through Jesus. In a statement that reflects the word found in John 3:16, our author writes that "God sent his only Son into the world that we might live through him" (vs. 9). Then, in verse 10, John tells us that God's love is revealed in God's decision to send the Son into the world to be the atoning sacrifice. Once again, the idea of atonement enters the conversation. John doesn't tell us how Jesus acts as an atoning sacrifice, only that his is the atoning sacrifice for our sins, as has already been revealed in 1 John 2:2. The cross isn't explicitly mentioned, but the cross would appear to be assumed here. Thus, not only is the incarnation a revelation of God's love, but so is Jesus' death, through which our sins are expiated or washed away. That is, God's love, as revealed to us in Jesus, is sacrificial—God is willing to give up everything so that we might once again experience oneness with God and with one another. Perhaps we might bring into the conversation Paul Tillich's definition of love: "Love is the drive towards the unity of the separated."[43] Whatever the atonement is, it serves to bring about the unity of the separated, beginning with the human-divine separation, and then the human to human separation. This is the ultimate expression of God's love for us—that we might be one with God and with each other through Christ—who is love in the flesh.

If we affirm that God is love and that Jesus is God's fullest expression of that love, then the next question has to do with the way in which we participate in that love. John suggests that God's love is reciprocal. We love because God first loved us. The question is: How do we, who are human, return love to a God who is

---

42  D. Moody Smith, *First, Second, and Third John (Interpretation: A Bible Commentary for Teaching and Preaching),* (Louisville: John Knox Press, 1991), p. 106.

43  Paul Tillich, *Love, Power and Justice: Ontological Analyses and Ethical Applications,* (London: Oxford University Press, 1954), p. 25.

invisible to us? It's one thing to say I love God, but what does that require of me? The answer is: we love the invisible God by loving the neighbor who is visible to us. Again, John makes clear that this is an embodied faith. So, when we love our neighbor, whom we can see, then God's love is perfected in us.

## ABIDING IN THE GOD WHO IS LOVE (13-16)

The declaration that God is love, and that those who know God, love one another is inextricably connected to John's continued emphasis on abiding in God. There is this reciprocal relationship with God. If we abide in God, God abides in us. This Johannine vision is linked with the presence of the Holy Spirit, who is given to God's people by God. As we have already discovered, not every spirit is from God. Therefore, we must test the spirits. The test is a doctrinal one, or so it seems (1 John 4:1-6). Once again, we encounter the dividing line between John's community and the community that left, the community that followed the spirit of the Antichrist. John invokes the authority of witness, declaring: "we have seen and do testify that the Father has sent his Son as the Savior of the World" (vs. 14). With this we return to the opening lines of the letter, where John declares "what we have seen with our eyes, what we have looked at and touched with our hands, concerning the word of life" (1 John 1:1).

While it might seem as if John has moved on from the discussion of love, the fact is, we haven't. To abide in God is to love God. Especially if we follow Tillich's definition, then to abide in God is to be reunited with God, and God with us. This abiding takes place in the context of our relationship with Jesus. God abides in those who confess Jesus as savior of the world. Eugene Peterson captures this vision well in the version of verses 15-16 in *The Message:* "Everyone who confesses that Jesus is God's Son participates continuously in an intimate relationship with God. We know it so well, we've embraced it heart and soul, this love that comes from

God." This is what it means to abide in God and God to abide in us—to be in intimate relationship.

In the second half of verse 16, we find one of the most definitive statements about love and its connection to God: "God is love, and those who abide in love abide in God, and God abides in them." Despite the explicitness of this statement, Thomas Jay Oord notes that love has seldom been put at the center of Christian theology. He writes:

> One might conclude that love actually lies "behind the curtain' of Christian theologies. Love is unseen and rarely mentioned, but love remains present nonetheless. Perhaps this is true in some cases. But I believe love should take theology's center stage."[44]

If love does take center stage, then what does that mean for Christians? Oord has further developed that idea that God is love, by speaking of this love being uncontrolling and noncoercive. That is, love precedes power, which leads to a redefinition of power.[45]

## No Fear of God (17-21)

If God is love, and Jesus is the fullest expression of God's love, a love that we reciprocate by loving our neighbor, then shouldn't love define the way we see the world? John answers that question be declaring that there is no fear in love. That is—fear is the opposite of love, and if we experience love then fear should not be present in our lives. As we ponder that vision, it is important that we remember that John makes this statement in a letter that expresses a very dualistic theology. There is a strong *us versus them* mentality present in the letter, which seems to run counter to this vision. Perhaps we would be wise to read the letter in light of this statement about fear and love.

---

44  Thomas Jay Oord, *The Nature of Love: A Theology,* (St. Louis: Chalice Press, 2010), p. 4.

45  Thomas Jay Oord, *The Uncontrolling Love of God: An Open and Relational Account of Providence,* (Downers Grove: IVP Academic, 2015), pp. 162-163.

When it comes to the topic of fear, we need to separate out the kind of fear discussed here from the kind of fear spoken of in Proverbs. In Proverbs, fear of God is the beginning of wisdom (Prov. 1:7). Fear of God is understood in Proverbs as reverence and awe, not terror, which is the more typical definition of fear. While, I may be dumbstruck when I'm in the presence of God, that is not because I fear being hit by lightning bolt. This isn't the Wizard of Oz, who is first met by Dorothy and her friends amid fire and noise. John envisions an intimate relationship between God and God's people, but that doesn't mean we're pals. While intimate and personal, it is also marked by a sense of awe and respect. Our relationship with God isn't a backslapping kind of friendship, but we needn't stand in fear of God, thinking that God is angry or malevolent.

I realize that the church has often taught something very different. Indeed, we can find texts, even in 1 John, that speak of wrath and anger and punishment, but if we take this confession seriously, that God is love, and that Jesus is the fullest expression of that love, then our portrayals of God must not focus on wrath and punishment. Many of us have heard or experienced messages of "Turn or burn." Indeed, Jonathan Edwards gave a famous sermon that spoke about "sinners in the hands of an angry God." Somehow, I cannot connect that kind of confession of faith with the confession that God is love or that there is no fear in love.

So, what does John mean when he declares that there is no fear in love? Or, that "perfect love casts out all fear." It would seem that John is inviting us to be bold in our service to God and humanity, because we have nothing to fear, except perhaps fear itself, since we abide in God's love.

And here is where the rubber meets the road. We live in a world that capitalizes on our fears. There are lots of fear mongers out there in the world, ready and willing to pounce. Politicians and pundits regularly point out why we should be afraid. The Department of Homeland Security was created after 9-11 to defend the homeland. They set up a color-coded system to let us know how much fear we should be feeling at any given moment, especially when we go to the airport. Everywhere we turn, we hear about the threat of terrorists blowing up planes and trains, or immigrants taking jobs from hard-working people. It makes for good politics, but not good religion.

While there are good reasons to be cautious in life, that is different from living in fear, which is contrary to love. John writes that fear is related to punishment. If we live in fear, then we have not yet reached perfection. If we live in fear, then our relationship with God remains immature.

It is most likely that John's community lived under duress. They faced a splinter group that may have been trying to undermine their community theologically. They also faced a hostile world, which threatened them with bodily harm due to their confession of faith in Jesus. In other words, they had much to fear. Our situation, at least in the West, is much different. And so perhaps we can take this vision of love and expand it to address the kinds of fear that we encounter in daily life. While there are good reasons to be cautious in life, that doesn't mean we should live our lives in fear that God will get us if we step out of line. When fear takes hold, love disappears. Fear divides, love unites. Fear makes us cynical and even paranoid, and paranoia has dangerous side effects. It can lead to exclusion and even violence, especially when it becomes part of a political ideology. The message here, then, is this: if we embrace the God who is love, as revealed to us in Jesus, then we should say no to fear. By saying no to fear, we can begin reaching out to the world, building bridges to those who are hurting and standing on the margins of society. Rooted in God's love, we will be united to those needing to experience reconciliation with God and with neighbor.

Love is rooted in relationship to God. "We love because he first loved us" (vs. 19). So, if you say you love God and hate your brothers or sisters, then you are a liar. Of course, this statement in verses 20-21 give evidence of John's dualism. There is no middle ground between love and hate. Again, it should be noted that in

1 John, the brother or sister, not the neighbor, is in view. At least in this context, as John lays it out amid serious division within the broader community, it is an internal kind of love. The question then is can we expand beyond John's more limited vision? Might we hear this not only to love those within the community, but to reach beyond the community. Of course, if we can't love those within the community, it will be difficult to love those living outside it.

## QUESTIONS FOR MEDITATION AND DISCUSSION

1.  In verses 1-6, John addresses his community, and tells them to test the spirits, because not every spirit is from God. As we turn to the next section, beginning in verse 7, we are introduced to a call to love one another, because God is love. Why is love of one another related to love of God?

2.  How does love relate to being born of God? How might this statement be related to Jesus' conversation with Nicodemus concerning being "born from above"? (John 3:3).

3.  While we don't have a full definition of love here, we are told in whom God's love is revealed. In whom is God's love revealed in the one sent by God? Do you see a similarity here with what is declared in John 3:16? With that in mind, how is love related to Jesus being the atoning sacrifice or expiation of our sins?

4.  Moving forward, why is loving one another a sign that God's love is perfected in us? Who is it that we are commanded to love? Those in the community or everyone?

5.  As we consider verses 13-16, do you see a change of focus? What is that focus and how might it relate to the conversation about love? What do you make of the call to confess Jesus as Son of God? How is this a sign that we abide in God? If we read verses 15-16 in Eugene Peterson's *The Message*, what does it mean to abide in God?

6.  Verse 16 seems to be a bridge between the conversation about abiding in God (16a), while the second half returns us to the focus on love. What is the message here concerning love?

7.  How is love perfected in us? What is the marker that love has been perfected?

8.  God is love, and we are to love one another. That message is clear. Now, in verse 18, John makes another declaration. What is fear and why is there no fear in love? How is this a marker that love has been perfected?

9.  As the chapter closes, John declares that one cannot love God and hate one's brother or sister. Do you see in this a sign of John's dualism? Can there be no middle ground between hate and love?

10. Having explored this section that focuses on love, how does this message fit within the broader message of John's letter? Do you have a different sense of this word about love now than before?

## EXERCISE:

In 1 John 4:18, John declares that there is no fear in love. Using a concordance, look up texts that speak of fear. What do you find there? How is fear related to love elsewhere in Scripture? Is the kind of fear noted here different from other forms of fear in Scripture? If love excludes fear, then why do we fear? Discuss your findings with others.

## A CALL TO PRAYER:

*We have heard John declare that love is your prime identity. May we live out of that love so that fear no longer defines our identity, but we might act boldly in love.*

# Session 8

## Overcoming the World

### 1 John 5:1-12

VISION:

1 John is best known for its declaration that God is love. In this lesson, we take note of the context in which John develops his theology of love. It is a reminder that the community is beleaguered and needing encouragement. Once again, we see John's dualistic theology at work, raising the question once again as to whether we can separate John's message from his dualistic vision.

READING: 1 JOHN 5:1-12

Please read the passage for the day in at least two different translations, a more formal translation, such as the NRSV, CEB, RSV, or NIV, and then read it again in a freer version or paraphrase such as *The Message*, *Phillip's*, or the *New Living Translation*. As you read, pay attention to images that warrant further exploration.

LESSON:

### Confronting the Domination System— Summarizing the Journey

Perhaps you can remember watching those old Western movies, the kind that John Wayne appeared in back in the forties and the fifties, back before Clint Eastwood's more complicated Westerns began to appear. In those movies of yesteryear, there were good guys and bad guys, and you always knew who was who. Sometimes, they even wore different colored hats—one white, one black—just so you didn't miss the point.

We call this dualism, and dualism lets us see everything in black and white, either/or terms. This is a zero-sum vision, in which you're either with us or against us. In this context, if you are against us, then you must be evil, and if you're evil then I may have to destroy you. We like to see ourselves living on the right side of things, which means that our opponents must be evil. American Presidents have spoken of perceived enemies in terms of evil empires or an axis of evil. Such images make sense to many, but is life this cut and dry? Perhaps Abraham Lincoln was right when he pointed out that both sides during the Civil War believed that they were on the side of truth, and both prayed to the same God for victory. Lincoln hoped he was on the side of God, but he was willing to admit the possibility that he was wrong.

John's vision of reality is starkly dualistic. You're either a child of God or a child of the devil. In John's mind, maybe because he's fighting for the survival of his community, there doesn't seem to be much room for any shades of gray. Even if we don't see things in the same black-and-white framework as John, we know that both good and evil are present in the world. In fact, both good and evil might be in each of us. Therefore, we have a responsibility to discern what is good and what is not, in order to make good choices in life.

It's in the context of this need to discern the truth that we encounter John's use of the word *kosmos,* which is Greek for world. While the gospel of John, which has a different author, speaks of God's love for the world (John 3:16), in this letter we hear about Jesus conquering and overcoming the *kosmos.* The author of 1 John speaks here of what some call "The System." Walter Wink calls this system "the Powers." It is hierarchical, racist, sexist, unjust and unfair. No matter how hard you work, you never can get off the treadmill. We sometimes call this the status quo, and the "powers that be" will defend themselves with everything at their disposal—including violence.

The good news, according to John, is that while God loves the creation, Jesus has defeated the "Domination System" by way of the cross. That is, Jesus took on the "Powers" that dominate our daily lives, the "system" that tries to keep us in our place, and defeated it on the cross. Unfortunately, history has demonstrated, that we've often failed to learn the lesson of the cross. Indeed, too often the church has blessed and even benefitted from the System. We've discovered that the temptation to become an extension of the state is strong. Remember that when Constantine decided to hitch his future to Christianity's rising star, the church was only too eager to join up. Once they agreed to work together, it didn't take long for the church to not only become an agent of the state and but also become corrupt.

Although church and state may be separate in America, history shows that even here the church can get sucked in by the system. Indeed, a recent survey suggests that the more people go to church, the more likely they are to support the use of torture to protect the nation's security. This is true, despite the fact that Jesus was himself tortured and killed by the state in the name of national security.

There is a message here for us: While the world relies on violence and oppression to achieve its purpose, Jesus has overcome that system through his own death. Unlike the system, Jesus embraced nonviolence and love, and while that led to his death, in the end he emerged victorious.

## Belief, Obedience, and Love (1 John 5:1-6)

As we read through 1 John, we have noticed that John places great emphasis on belief, obedience, and love. All three fit together. If you believe, you will obey, and obedience to God leads to love of God and love of one another. We've been reminded that God is love and that those who abide in God will love one another. John doesn't speak of loving one's neighbor, which leaves open the question of how broad one's love should be. For John, Christian identity is rooted in the confession that Jesus is the Son of God and that he came in the flesh. If one believes this to be true, then on is born of God. That makes God our parent, and those who love the parent love the child (1 John 5:1).

When we hear the word belief, it is important that we understand that John has in mind more than intellectual assent. Belief here goes with obedience, for belief is a commitment to live for and with Jesus. That belief is expressed by obedience to God's commandment, which is described in chapter 3. God's commandment is this: we should believe in the name of his Son Jesus Christ and love one another. Fortunately for us, according to John, these commandments are not burdensome for those who are born of God. If one is born of God, then one will conquer the world. To conquer the world is to believe that Jesus is the Son of God.

In speaking of conquering the world, John likely would have us look back to Jesus' own statement regarding his conquest of the world. As he was preparing to go to the cross, Jesus gathers his disciples, and offers them a word of encouragement. He tells them: "I have said this to you, so that in me you may have peace. In the world you face persecution. But take courage; *I have conquered the world!*" (John 16:33). John's community is facing persecution in some fashion, but he would have them remember that Jesus has already conquered the world by way of the cross. What does it mean for this community, that having been born of God, they have conquered the world? D. Moody Smith suggests that "those who have conquered the world have risen above it so that it no longer taints or influences, much less determines them. They have successfully fulfilled the injunction of 1 John 2:15: 'Do not love the world or the things of the world.'"[46]

When we read a passage like this, which speaks of conquering the world, we can read it in an overly-spiritualized fashion in which we separate ourselves completely from the world. We could choose what some have called the "Benedict Option," and construct a monastic vision in which we shut ourselves off from the culture around us. This is what H. Richard Niebuhr called "Christ against Culture." As Niebuhr puts it: "hence the loyalty of the believer is directed entirely toward the new order, the new society and its Lord."[47] There is much to commend about the vision that some

---

46   D. Moody Smith, *First, Second, and Third John, (Interpretation: A Bible Commentary for Teaching and Preaching)*, (Louisville: John Knox Press, 1991), p. 119.

47   H. Richard Niebuhr, *Christ and Culture*, (New York: Harper Torchbooks, 1951), p. 48.

have maintained, down through the ages, about keeping Christ and Caesar separate. Reform has often been the result of such visions. At the same time, such a position has its own problems. So, as we reflect on John's declaration, what is the proper relationship to culture? Niebuhr offers a word of guidance that keeps things in balance:

> The movement of withdrawal and renunciation is a necessary element in every Christian life, even though it be followed by an equally necessary movement of responsible engagement in cultural tasks.[48]

In other words, even though God would not have us be defined by the world's values, as Niebuhr reminds us, we make use of the culture in which we abide. We use its language and customs, philosophies and resources. We live in the world, but we're not of the world. Finding that balance is not easy, but necessary.

## Witnesses to the Son of God (1 John 5:6-12).

The one who conquers the world is the one who believes that Jesus is the Son of God (vs. 5). This Jesus came, John declares, with water and blood, not the water only. To this truth, the Spirit bears witness. What is the meaning of John's words? Is this reference to water and blood a reference to baptism and the Eucharist? Or, does John have in mind Jesus' human birth, as opposed to only a spiritual/non-corporeal birth? In his translation of the passage, Eugene Peterson takes the water to mean baptism, but he interprets the blood as a reference to Jesus' sacrificial death (as opposed to the Eucharist, which is something never mentioned in 1 John). This leads Peterson to insist in verse 8 that baptism, crucifixion, and the Spirit all agree that Jesus is the Son of God. What then does John have in mind here?

The references in verses 6-8 to water, blood, and Spirit present us with certain problems. Since neither baptism nor Eucharist are mentioned in 1 John, it would seem odd to bring them in to the

---

48  Niebuhr, *Christ and Culture*, p. 68.

conversation at the end of the letter. Nonetheless this is a common interpretation of the phrase. On the other hand, birth language fits the context and is common to John's message. Thus, the emphasis on water and blood could be a reference to the birth process. That would reinforce John's concern to emphasize the humanity of Jesus, whereas the water by itself might speak of a more spiritual, non-corporeal reality. As Jaime Clark Soles puts it: "By insisting on this earthy, earthly, wet, and bloody reality that Jesus experienced, the author may be emphasizing his actual death, thus countering once again a docetic Christology that insists that Jesus only 'seemed' human."[49] This does seem to make sense of the context, for John is insistent that despite the suggestion that Jesus is divine in some way, Jesus is fully human.

In John's mind, there are three compelling witnesses—the Spirit, the water, and the blood. While the original reader may have understood John's intentions here, as for us, as Raymond Brown suggests, there "is the utter obscurity of what he is talking about."[50] Then, in verse nine, John declares that "if we receive testimony, the testimony of God is greater." As to the nature of this human testimony, John does not reveal anything. However, God's testimony is greater. It could be that John has in mind the testimony of John the Baptist, which, according to the Gospel of John, was superseded by Jesus' ministry. Jesus' witness is confirmed by having been sent by the Father (John 5:31-38).

John goes on to speak of the testimony that is in the heart of one believes (vs. 10). If you believe then you take the testimony of God to heart, which I take to mean that believing that testimony is transformative. On the other hand, if one does not believe, then one calls God a liar. To believe the testimony of God leads to eternal life in God's Son. If one believes, one has life. If one does not believe that Jesus is the Son of God, then one does not have life. Again, we

---

49   Jaime Clark Soles, "1, 2, 3 John," in *Fortress Commentary on the Bible: Two Volume Set,* Gale A. Yee, Ed., (Minneapolis: Fortress Press), (Kindle Locations 56902-56903).

50   Raymond Brown, *Epistles of John (Anchor Bible),* (Garden City, NY: Doubleday and Co.), p. 595.

see the stark contrast between two visions: one vision leads to life, the other to death. There is no middle ground, no room for gray. There is sadness in this closing, but John wants us to understand the consequences of belief and unbelief.

## QUESTIONS FOR MEDITATION AND DISCUSSION

1. As we come to chapter 5, we near the end of our study of 1 John. This letter is marked by a strong dualism. What are the implications of this dualism? Where do you find examples of dualism in our culture—movies, literature, etc.?

2. The chapter under review opens with the declaration that everyone who believes that Jesus is the Christ or Messiah is born of God. How might belief lead to being born of God in 1 John?

3. John returns to the topic of love, which along with belief and obedience is of central importance in this letter, how is love understood here? What is the relationship of love of God and love of one another? Do you see the call to love one another applying outside the community or only inside it? Why?

4. John returns to the idea of obedience to God's commands. What is the nature of obedience here in 1 John 5? How does obedience lead to conquering the world? Why do we need to conquer the world? What is it about the world that must be conquered?

5. Following up on this call to conquer the world, theologian H. Richard Niebuhr, in his classic study *Christ and Culture*, suggests that 1 John represents the model of "Christ against Culture?" What does Niebuhr understand by this designation? Is it feasible? Or, must we find another way of relating to culture? (see *Christ and Culture*, p. 68).

6.  In verse 6, we move on from conquering the world to the witnesses or testimonies toward God. What are the three primary witnesses and on what do they agree? (1 John 5:6-8).

7.  What might John mean by the witnesses of water and blood? What are some of the options, and how do you understand them?

8.  John notes that if one is willing to accept human testimony, why not accept the testimony of God? Why might that testimony by greater than human testimony? How might this statement be understood in light of what we reading John 5:31-38? Could the contrast made here be a reflection on the witness of John the Baptist?

9.  Where does receiving the witness of God lead? What should we make of this rather dualistic word about life and not life?

## EXERCISE:

The reference to the witness of the water and blood is ambiguous. Using commentaries, such as Raymond Brown's and D. Moody Smith's, explore the possible interpretations of these two witnesses. What might John have meant by these words, and what are the implications of the different interpretations. Share these interpretations and the implications for the church with your group.

## A CALL TO PRAYER:

*We have received your testimony through the work of the Spirit, testified through blood and water, eucharist and baptism, of the truth that eternal life is given through Christ the Lord.*

# SESSION 9

## PRAYERS OF RESTORATION
### 1 John 5:13-21

## VISION:

With this lesson we bring the study of 1 John to a close. We learn more fully why the letter, if it was a letter, was written. We also receive a strong call to pray and to live fully the Christian life. As we bring the letter to a close, how might we bring this message to life in our context, recognizing that John speaks often in dualistic terms?

## READING: 1 JOHN 5:13-21

Please read the passage for the day in at least two different translations, a more formal translation, such as the NRSV, CEB, RSV, or NIV, and then read it again in a freer version or paraphrase such as *The Message*, *Phillip's*, or the *New Living Translation*. As you read, pay attention to images that warrant further exploration.

## LESSON:

### Purpose of Writing – 1 John 5:13

We are coming to the end of this document we call 1 John. Whether it is a letter or not, it speaks to the concerns of a community caught in the midst of what they perceived to be a spiritual battle between God and the Evil One. The author casts an eschatological vision of the world in which cosmic forces are at war, and yet the author wants the community to know that because they believe in Jesus, they have conquered the world (1 John 5:4). There might be battles raging, but the victory has been achieved.

In verse 13, John writes what appears to be the closing sentence of his letter: "I write these things to you who believe in the name of the Son of God, so that you may know that you have eternal life." This statement takes us back to the beginning of the letter, where in 1 John 1:4, John declares: "We are writing these things so that our joy may be complete." There is no explicit word here about how their joy is to be made complete, but joy would be the result of experiencing eternal life in Jesus.

The closing declaration closely parallels the last verse of John 20 (John 20:31), which seems bring the Gospel of John to a conclusion (despite the presence of the epilogue in John 21). The author of the Gospel writes: "But these are written so that you may come to believe that Jesus is the Messiah, the Son of God, and that through believing you may have life in his name." In both passages, one from the letter and one from the Gospel, the authors of the texts make a declaration of purpose, and both statements declare that they write so that the recipients might believe in Jesus, and thus receive eternal life. As for the closing verses of 1 John, they seem to flow out of this closing statement. Unlike John 21, these verses are directly related to the message found in 1 John 5:13, for they speak to belief in the Son of God and eternal life. Speaking of this concluding word, Raymond Brown writes:

He wishes to strengthen readers in their Christology since only a faith that is correct christologically gives life. Throughout the work his attacks on the secessionists have been provoked by the danger they presented by proselytizing his adherents. He has struggled to prevent further erosion among those adherents, and he draws his work to an end by stressing the positive values of their Community of faith.[51]

What follows expands the message stated clearly in verse 13, beginning in verse 14 and 15 with a commendation of their faith, which is strong enough that they can boldly approach God with their prayers.

---

51   Raymond Brown, *Epistles of John (Anchor Bible)*, (Garden City, NY: Doubleday and Co., 1982), p. 632.

## Bold Prayers—1 John 5:14-15

In verses 14-15, John encourages the readers to be bold in their prayers, because if they ask anything "according to his will," then God will hear their prayers. The translation of verse 14 in the *Common English Bible* speaks of confidence, while the NRSV speaks of boldness. In either case, this confidence in God allows the people of God to ask whatever they wish, if asked "according to his will." When prayers are offered in this manner, then "we know that we have received what we asked from him" (1 John 5:15 CEB). This declaration is like that which is found in John 14, where Jesus declares: "If in my name you ask me for anything, I will do it" (John 14:14).

When we read a passage like this one in 1 John 5, or its parallel in John 14, it is possible to read it in terms of a prosperity gospel. If you believe you receive. Such is not the case here. John isn't encouraging the members of the community to claim a big house or a new car for themselves. To do so would be to live out of worldly values, and John is quite clear that this community of believers has conquered the world (1 John 5:5). What is asked for and received is revealed in verse 13. This would be the promise of eternal life. It would also, it seems, refer to the prayers offered for members of the community, as revealed in verses 16-17.

## Prayers for Sinners—1 John 5:16-17

John reminds his readers that if they ask according to God's will, then they will receive from God what they ask. This leads to a conversation about prayers on behalf of sinners. John cautions the readers to keep in mind that there are different kinds of sin. Some forms lead to death and cannot be rectified by one's prayers. This would not be according to God's will. Remember, at the heart of these prayers is the promise of eternal life. So, John invites the reader to offer prayers for those who commit sins that do not lead to death. That is, it is appropriate to pray for someone who has not committed a "mortal sin," and these prayers will be effectual in restoring that person to right relationship with God. As for those, who commit "mortal sins," there is no real reason to pray for them.

John regularly declares that those who are born of God do not sin, yet John also recognizes that we do sin. This is why John speaks of Jesus being the advocate who is the atoning sacrifice for the sins of the world (1 John 2:1-2). So, if we see someone sinning, perhaps straying from the path of righteousness, it is appropriate to pray that they would be restored to that pathway. We can do this with confidence, because we make the request in accordance with God's will. Unfortunately, there are some whose sins lead to death. These mortal sins cannot be rectified by our prayers. The assumption here is that a mortal sin excludes one from eternal life. If one commits such a sin, there is no point of praying a prayer of intercession for such a person.

So, what is this mortal sin? In Roman Catholic tradition, there are two forms of sin—mortal and venial. Venial sins are less serious breaches of the divine law, and one can pray for another to be restored from such a sin. Mortal sins, on the other hand, are serious—sins such as murder and adultery. In this case, this mortal sin appears to be apostasy. Those who commit this sin refuse to confess that Jesus is the Christ come in the flesh. In doing this, they have effectively cut themselves off from the community of believers, and thus they cut themselves off from eternal life. If one refuses to confess, then that person cannot be prayed into the realm of God. They have already chosen their fate. So, pray for brothers and sisters, those within the community, who have stumbled in their journey. Pray they will find their way back on to the path of righteousness. As for those who left the community and refuse to confess Jesus, they have chosen their own pathway—the path of the Evil One. In John's mind there is no need to pray for them. As to why he would direct their prayers this way, it would seem that John wants to make sure that the community of believers is not contaminated by the false message of the secessionists. As Raymond Brown puts it: "while this may strike us as bigoted and scarcely Christian, it stands in a lineage of OT references to sins too heinous to pray about and NT references to the sin against the Holy Spirit that will not be forgiven. It is a logical (even if unhappy) reflection of Johannine dualism in which 'the world lies in the grasp of the Evil One,' so that if one does not belong to God, one belongs to the devil by choice (1 John 5:19)."[52]

## Living as Children of God—1 John 5:18-21

Beginning in verse 18 John makes three statements that begin with "we know." First, "we know that those who are born of God do not sin" (vs. 18a). The second statement declares: "We know that we are God's children" (vs. 19a). The third statement declares: "we know that the Son of God has come and has given us understanding so that we may know him who is true" (vs. 20). As he concludes this epistle, John wants the community to remember what they already know, what has been known from the beginning and shared with them (1 John 1:1-4).

John first declaration concerns the status of those born of God. He writes: "*We know* that those who are born of God do not sin." While this may seem unrealistic, perhaps John isn't speaking of a static state of sinlessness, but instead is referring to a pattern. To be born of God means that one does not continue in sin. As D. Moody Smith suggests, we might translate 18 as "We know that everyone who is born of God does not continue in sin, but the one who was begotten [or born] of God [i.e., Jesus] is keeping him, and the evil one is not touching him." By translating the present tense verbs in "their full, continuative sense" the present state of Christians is emphasized, without "creating the impression that freedom from sin is a kind of automatic process that removes them from the realm of any meaningful moral decision."[53] In other words, if one is born of God, one's life is not determined or dominated by sin, because Jesus is there to protect them. The children of God

---

52  Brown, *Epistles of John*, p. 636.
53  D. Moody Smith, *First, Second, and Third John (Interpretation: A Bible Commentary for Teaching and Preaching)*, (Louisville: John Knox Press, 1991), p. 136.

are protected from the assault of the Evil One, because they live
within the circle of God's protection. That circle is the community.
In John's mind, the community has strong walls, that prevent the
Evil One from infiltrating. Such a vision of the church might be
off-putting to modern sensibilities. Many of us would prefer to
focus on the center, rather than the boundaries. However, for John
and his community, the danger posed by the secessionists required
them to circle the wagons and keep the Evil One at bay. While we
might wish to keep the doors open to all, John does offer us a word
of caution. Not every ideology or vision is appropriate to the community of faith. John uses a doctrinal rule to guide the community.
That kind of rule has become problematic in the modern context,
but perhaps we would do well to consider questions of identity in
Christ, and ponder how to balance openness with fidelity to God's
vision of the realm.

The second "we know" concerns one's identity as a child of
God. John writes: "*We know* that we are God's children, and that
the whole world lies under the power of the evil one." Again, we see
John's dualism at work. On one side of the line is the community
of believers composed of God's children. John affirms them in their
confidence in their status as children of God. On the other side of
the line is the world, which "lies under the power of the evil one."
John's concern is that the world that lies under the power of the
evil one might be gaining a foothold in the community, that is, the
danger posed by the secessionists and their counter message. This
message isn't unique to John. It fits closely with the vision expressed
by the community that created the Dead Sea Scrolls.[54]

The third "we know" appears in verse 20: "And *we know* that
the Son of God has come and has given us understanding so that
we may know him who is true; and we are in him who is true, in
his Son Jesus Christ. He is the true God and eternal life." The Son
of God, that is Jesus the Christ, provides understanding so that we
might know him who is true. That would be God. We are in the
one who is true and in his Son Jesus Christ. There is in this rather

---

54  Brown, *Epistles of John,* p. 639.

complex statement a sense that if we abide in Christ, we abide in God, and God abides in us. We know this to be true, because the Son has revealed it to us. One of the key elements here is that we need not ascend into heaven to gain this knowledge; rather the Son descends to give us this knowledge. There is in this statement covenantal vocabulary, for the way in which John envisions knowing God reflects the covenant language of Jeremiah (Jeremiah 31:31-34). There is in this knowledge not just intellectual understanding, but true intimacy. Considering the role that Jesus plays in this, John can speak of him as "true God and eternal life" (vs. 20). This raises the question as to the degree that John is embracing the idea of Jesus' divinity. It's likely not in the Nicaean sense, but at the very least it provides fodder for future development. Raymond Brown offers this summation that is worth considering: "The fact that both GJohn (20:28) and I John end by confessing Jesus as God shows how important this was in Johannine thought and not simply in an abstract way, for in each case the confession of Jesus as God is followed by a mention of the (eternal) life that such belief brings to his followers."[55]

These three statements of "we know" are a strong reminder of what is at stake. John is concerned about the future of his community and wants to strengthen their resolve as they face the separatists who continue to refuse to acknowledge that the Son of God has come in the flesh. But, if they continue in their belief, which is more than mere intellectual assent, in Jesus, thereby staying true to the covenant that God has made with them through Jesus, then they will experience eternal life.

The letter ends with a brief but powerful statement: "Little children, keep yourselves from idols." That seems like a fairly negative way to end a document, but it might be a helpful one, not only for the original reader, but also for the modern reader. Thinking in terms of the original reader, this statement would be, as Raymond Brown suggests, the "negative counterpart of the three positive affirmations in 5:18-20." He points to the covenant nature of this

55  Brown, *Epistles of John*, p. 640.

statement, with the statement about idols being "understood in terms of the secession." Thus, as Brown puts it: "In the author's judgment, the secessionists are trying to seduce his adherents to leave the covenanted Community and its understanding of the God who was revealed in Jesus Christ come in the flesh, and to adopt a false life-style in which commandments are not important and sin is not a source of worry."[56] To go after idols would be to go after the secessionists. What then would be the idols that we face today? What seeks to draw us away from our confession of faith in the God revealed in Jesus? Jaime Clark-Soles asks that very question, and offers a few possibilities for us to consider: "Do wealth, status, power, ego, vanity, and nationalism qualify? Are there other false teachings or gods that tempt people away from God?"[57]

## QUESTIONS FOR MEDITATION AND DISCUSSION

1.  We have come to the end of 1 John. The remaining verses form a conclusion to this document. Verse 13 offers what seems to be a concluding statement that restates the author's purpose for writing. What is that purpose? Turning to John 20:31, do you see any similarities? What are they, and how might the similarities undergird the relationship of the two documents?

2.  In verses 14-15, John begins to flesh out his purpose in writing the letter. In these verses, John speaks of prayer. What does John say about prayer? How should we approach our prayers? What is it John would have us request?

3.  If eternal life is the appropriate request in our prayers, when we turn to verses 16-17, we find John speaking to two kinds of situations. In one situation, prayer is effectual. In the other it is not. What might we learn from this passage about the value

---

56  Brown, *Epistles of John,* p. 640-641.
57  Jaime Clark-Soles, "1, 2, 3 John," in *Fortress Commentary on the Bible: Two Volume Set,* Gail Yee, ed., (Kindle Locations 56991-56992). Minneapolis: Fortress Press. Kindle Edition.

of intercessory prayer, especially when it comes to restoring a sinning brother or sister to fellowship?

4.   While there are those, whom we can effectually pray for, there are others for whom John recommends that we not pray. This is the sin that is mortal. What might this sin be? Why should we not pray for such a person?

5.   If this mortal sin is apostasy or idolatry, why would this sin lead to death? What does this say about the danger of apostasy in John's mind? Who might John be thinking of?

6.   When we arrive at verses 18-20, we will notice three "we know" statements (18a, 19a, 20). What are these three statements? What message should we know?

7.   What should we know about those who are born of God and sin?

8.    What do we know as God's children?

9.   What understanding has the Son of God come to give us? What does it mean to know the one who is true and that we are in the one who is true?

10. Not only does John reveal that the Son of God brings understanding of the one who is true, but he seems to suggest that Jesus is "the true God and eternal life." What does John seem to be saying about Jesus, if, as many believe, this statement is being applied to Jesus?

11.  The purpose for writing is to enable the reader to experience eternal life. What might it mean that Jesus is called eternal life here?

12.  John's message concludes with what appears to be a rather negative statement: "Little children, keep yourselves from idols." What idols might John have in mind? If the idol is the

message of the secessionists, what is the nature of this idol? Why would John call on the community to avoid such an idol?

13. What are the idols that we face in our contemporary situation?

14. As this is the final section of 1 John, what message do you take from this conversation? How might we bring John's message into the contemporary situation? Where might we find it difficult to do this?

## EXERCISE:

John brings up the idea of mortal sins. Using a theological dictionary, look up sin and research how the idea of mortal sin came to be understood over time, especially as the Roman Catholic Church distinguished between venial and mortal sins. Share your findings and discuss ways in which sin is understood in our contemporary age. Do we take sin as seriously as previous ages? Is this positive or negative?

## A CALL TO PRAYER:

*As we live in your presence, may we live boldly our faith, letting go of the things that bind us, so that we might express in our lives the love we read of here in 1 John.*

# SESSION 10

## WALKING IN OBEDIENCE

### 2 John

VISION:

2 John offers us a brief summation of what we discover in 1 John. There is an emphasis on obedience, love, and faithfulness to the message. Thus, the emphasis on walking in obedience to Christ and to God's commandments. Regarding faithfulness to the Christian message, the writer, now identified as the Elder, warns against welcoming into one's house or community those who bring a message contrary to the one given through the Elder. Set against the command to love, how should we understand what seems to be a rather inhospitable vision? This question will allow us to consider how open the community should be to differing views and practices. Is there a limit of what is permissible and acceptable?

READING: 2 JOHN

Please read the passage for the day in at least two different translations, a more formal translation, such as the NRSV, CEB, RSV, or NIV, and then read it again in a freer version or paraphrase such as *The Message, Phillip's,* or the *New Living Translation.* As you read, pay attention to images that warrant further exploration.

LESSON:

### Authorship and Destination—2 John 1-3

Besides being briefer that 1 John, unlike 1 John, 2 John takes on the traditional marks of a letter. It has a greeting or salutation and a closing. The author of the later is named (the Elder), as is the recipient (the Elect Lady). As to the identity of the Elder and the Elect Lady, there has been much speculation, and no firm answers. Tradition suggests that the author is John, son of Zebedee, an apostle of Jesus. The question then is why, if this is the Apostle, the author uses the title Elder. Ultimately, we do not know the name or provenance of the letter. As to the recipient, the reference to the "Elect Lady" is also ambiguous, leading to debates as to whether this is a letter written to an individual woman or to a congregation. Most scholars opt for the latter, which makes better sense of the material at hand.

Whether the two books have the same author is also a matter of discussion, though 2 John shares many of the same characteristics of the first letter, recapping the primary issues and concerns—obedience to the command to love and confession of Jesus as coming in the flesh—while addressing a particular issue—whether to welcome those who share a different message into the community. This discussion might prove useful in discerning how to create healthy boundaries in a congregation that seeks to be open to all.

The greeting comes from the elder, whose identity remains clouded, to the elect lady (*eklektē kyria*) and her children. The name given to the recipient is intriguing. There has been some consideration of the idea that this is a proper name, either *Electa* or *Kyria*. While such an idea is intriguing—because it would highlight the possibility of women's leadership in the early church—context suggests otherwise. That this designation might refer to a church makes more sense of the context, and it reflects the tendency that goes back to ancient times to think of nations, institutions, and communities as feminine. Considering the patriarchal nature of that society, this is not surprising. Consider the way in which the author of Ephesians describes the relationship between Christ and the church, with Christ being the groom and the church the bride (Ephesians 5:32).[58]

---

58    Raymond Brown, *The Epistles of John (Anchor Bible)*, (Garden City, NY: Doubleday & Co., 1982), p. 654.

The word *elect* is also important here. If the church is the "elect lady," then what does it mean for the church to be the elect? The way the Elder writes this, it suggests that this election is corporate not individual. The fact that the designation "elect lady" lacks a definite article may suggest that this is a circular letter, sent to all the congregations affiliated with the Elder. They are elect, because they are chosen by God, and those who are members of the congregation are the children of the elect lady. They are incorporated into the chosen community as they join with it. Thus, it is the church that is chosen, perhaps chosen to be God's vehicle of salvation.

If this is a congregation, as most scholars believe, the elder, whomever that might be, speaks in terms of loving in truth to those who know the truth. Truth becomes a key point in the discussion in light of the elder's dualistic vision. As we will see as we proceed, the elder is concerned about the possible influence of those he calls the antichrists. Note the use of the word "abide" together with truth. This truth "is in us and will be with us forever." In the Johannine community, truth has definite Christological implications. As D. Moody Smith notes, "'In the truth' here is the Johannine equivalent of Paul's 'in Christ.' 'All who know the truth' really means all who know the truth of God that is incarnate in Jesus Christ, as the following clause (vs. 2) shows. What is said of the truth here applies exactly to Jesus Christ."[59] Thus, to say that the truth abides in them is to say that Christ abides in them. That will be important as we move further into the letter.

As for the greeting that continues in verse 3, it is interesting that the Elder speaks in such confident terms. He writes that "grace, mercy, and peace will be with us from God the Father and from Jesus Christ, the Father's Son." There is no hint of doubt here. If you are part of the community, then you will have grace, mercy, and peace." That is because the Elder is confident that the Truth (Christ) dwells within the community and its members. The reference to

---

59   D. Moody Smith, *First, Second, and Third John (Interpretation: A Bible Commentary for Teaching and Preaching)*, (Louisville: John Knox Press, 1991), p. 140.

God the Father and Jesus Christ the Father's Son," offers at the very least hints of a binitarian vision of God, where Jesus shares in the Father's divinity. This is the only place in the New Testament where Jesus is spoken of as the "Son of the Father." [60]

## Walking in Truth and Love—2 John 4-6

The Elder writes with boundless joy to the Lady, because he knows that some of the Lady's children (members of the congregation) are walking in the Truth. While the use of the word "some" opens up questions about the others, it might simply be that the Elder speaks of those about whom he has knowledge. But, the Elder's confidence suggests, according to Raymond Brown, that "the secession, while a danger, has not yet torn the church apart." They are walking in the Truth, as they had been commanded. But, the danger is there. Perhaps not everyone in the church is at the same place with the truth. After all, the letter itself serves as a warning to the congregation.

In verse 5, the Elder turns to a commandment laid out in 1 John. This commandment calls on the congregation to love one another. The Elder encourages obedience to this commandment, which is not new. In fact, it is from the beginning. Then in verse 6, the Elder defines this love which the members are to show one another. Love involves walking according to God's commandments, which had been known from the beginning. The reference to walking is in reference to the Christian life being a pathway. To be a Christian is more than simply believing something, it involves a way of life. If, as it appears here, the Truth is Jesus, and Jesus is the Truth, then to walk in the Truth (verse 4) and to "walk according to the commandments" is to walk (live) as Jesus walks (lives).

## Be on Guard Against Deceivers—2 John 7-11

With verse seven we get to the heart of the letter—the statement of concern for the future of the community. The Elder warns the congregation about the "many deceivers [who] have gone out

---

60  Brown, *Epistles of John,* p. 659.

into the world." These are the ones who "do not confess that Jesus Christ has come in the flesh." These persons are the ones the Elder calls the antichrist (vs. 7). While the Elder spoke of his great joy at those who walked in the truth, not everyone did so. The reference here is surely to the secession, those who had left the community (as we read about in 1 John 4). Their deceit is marked by their refusal to confess that Jesus came in the flesh.

There is an eschatological element to this warning. While the NRSV and CEB translate the statement about making the confession that Jesus has come in the flesh as if it is a past event, Raymond Brown notes that the verb is present-tense. Therefore, we should read verse 7 as "For many deceivers have gone out into the world, men who do not confess Jesus Christ coming in the flesh."[61] The deception concerns a docetic form of Christology, that denies the embodiment of Jesus—that is, the full incarnation John stresses (John 1:14). The Elder is concerned about the community facing future judgment. They don't want to "lose what we have worked for but may receive a full reward." Thus, the warning, as Brown suggests: "If the secessionists come and lead them astray by false teaching about Christ, they will lose the very basis for such a reward."[62]

Then in verse 9, we have another warning. This time the warning concerns going beyond the teaching of Christ. As we saw in 1 John, the secessionists seem to offer a more progressive vision, one that goes above and beyond what was revealed and understood from the beginning (1 John 1:1-3). Those who remain true to what was revealed in the beginning, abide in Christ. Those who secede, go beyond Christ. That makes them antichrist. In the struggle against the Nazi's and the perversions of the German Christians, Dietrich Bonhoeffer pointed to the message of 2 John 9 in response to the attempts made by the German Christians to integrate Nazi ideology with the Christian faith. He wrote:

---

61   Brown, *Epistles of John,* p. 645, 686.
62   Brown, *Epistles of John,* p. 687.

A congregation that no longer takes seriously its separation from false teaching no longer takes truth seriously, that is, it does not take salvation seriously, and ultimately that means it does not take itself seriously, regardless of how pious or how well organized it is. Those who obey false teachers, and even promote and encourage them, are no longer obedient to Christ.[63]

The Elder considers the secessionists to be purveyors of false teaching, which if it is embraced, has eternal consequences. That false teaching is one that is not rooted in the person and teachings of Jesus.

When we move to verses 10 and 11, we encounter a specific word of guidance. That word has to do with giving hospitality to those who go beyond the teachings of Jesus. Do not welcome them into your homes, the Elder writes, because if you do, you participate in their evil deeds. This word about restricting welcome again runs counter to other words about hospitality in Scripture. Consider the word given in Hebrews about welcoming the stranger: "Do not neglect to show hospitality to strangers, for by doing that some have entertained angels without knowing it" (Hebrews 13:2). Again, context is important.

As we saw in 1 John, the Elder (if the same author, or at least within the same community of churches), there is a concern about the danger of an invasion of the church by the secessionists designed to lead them astray. The concern here is with the possibility that the community might be contaminated by false teaching. It's a bit like putting up a firewall to prevent one's computer from being hacked. So, in a context in which hospitality plays such a vital role, a warning goes up. Don't receive everybody. Test them to see if they bring the appropriate Christology.

While much of 2 John is derivative from what we encountered in 1 John, this case-study has implications for the contemporary

---

63   Dietrich Bonhoeffer *Theological Education Underground: 1937-1940 (Dietrich Bonhoeffer Works, volume 15)*, Victoria J. Barnett, ed., (Minneapolis: Fortress Press, 2012), p. 433.

church, especially churches that seek to be open, inclusive, and welcoming. In the face of so much bigotry and intolerance in the broader community, how do we hear a word from God in this passage of scripture. D. Moody Smith suggests that "perhaps the unique feature of this letter is best left unheeded, namely, the warning not to show hospitality or even friendliness to those who espouse false doctrine and do not walk in love. Shunning may still be practiced by the Amish, but it is not a good odor in modern society or modern churches. . .. Incivility neither has, nor needs, defenders."[64] I would think that most readers of this study would agree with Smith's assessment. However, especially in congregations that focus more on the center (Christ) than on borders, could there be something of value to be discussed regarding boundaries. What is and what is not acceptable? As Jaime Clark-Soles suggests, "our reading of 2 John today may evoke important questions about how to maintain group cohesion and draw healthy boundaries when destructive persons are allowed to wreak havoc on a community with impunity."[65]

So, when and how do we set boundaries in an inclusive community? Bonhoeffer could not remain within the official church, which had embraced a foreign ideology that denied Christ. In our context, what about harmful ideologies such as racism, xenophobia, sexism, as well as anti-LGBTQ sentiments? This passage, though it seems so contrary to our modern sensibilities might offer us an opportunity for conversation about what is appropriate and what is not? In the end, the question before us concerns how seriously we take our faith and the glue that keeps us together. It is good to remember why the Confessing Church put such a premium on Christology. In the Barmen Declaration, written by Karl Barth, among others, the church was called upon to affirm the lordship of Jesus and not that of the Nazis. What is our ultimate allegiance?

---

64 Smith, *First, Second, and Third John*, pp. 146-147.
65 Jaime Clark-Soles, "1, 2, 3 John," in Gale A. Yee. *Fortress Commentary on the Bible: Two Volume Set* (Kindle Locations 57064-57065). Fortress

## Final Greetings—2 John 12-13

The Elder ends his letter by revealing that he has much more to say, but that he would "rather not use paper and ink." He wanted to keep the letter brief and not waste a lot of paper writing things that are best left to face-to-face conversation. With that said, he shared his desire to be with them in person, so that his joy would be made complete (vs. 12). By revealing that he has more to say raises questions about the relationship of this letter to 1 John. Could this mean that 2 John actually preceded 1 John, and thus the latter could have been written because the Elder wasn't able to be with them. Or, was there more to say that what is revealed in 1 John. It is clear that the opening parts of this letter recap what we read in 1 John; what we don't know is whether the feared schism has already taken place or not. On the other hand, could it be that the Elder has confidential matters to discuss that are best left to direct conversation and not put down on paper. Or could this simply be the Elder's way of closing the letter? Whatever the reason for making this declaration, it's clear that the Elder wishes to be reunited with the recipients so that their joy might be made complete.

Then the letter ends in verse 13, with a reference to the "children of your elect sister" wanting to send greetings. This reference to "your elect sister" serves as an appropriate closure to a letter addressed to the "elect lady." We speak at times of sister churches (as we do sister cities), and such might be the case here. So, perhaps the Elder speaks as a member of or leader of the "elect sister," writing to another community of faith with which it is connected. As Raymond Brown puts it: "This constitutes and inclusion that dramatizes the family relationship among believers, whose status as children flows from there having been begotten by God (John 1:12-13)."[66] That opens up a conversation about the relationship of congregations to each other, and Christians with one another beyond the walls of the congregation.

---

66  Brown, *Epistles of John,* p. 696.

## QUESTIONS FOR MEDITATION AND DISCUSSION

1. What do you notice from a quick glance at this letter? What does its brevity suggest?

2. In verses 1-2, we read the greeting or salutation of the letter. What does it tell us about the author and the recipient?

   A. What do you make of the reference to the "elect lady?"

   B. There is a word here about Truth. What is this Truth that abides in us?

3. As the greeting continues in verse 3, from whom does grace, mercy, and peace derive from? What does the Elder say about God and Jesus, and their relationship?

4. Reading verses 4-6, the Elder writes about being overjoyed with the knowledge that some walk in truth, and encourages walking according to the commandments. What does the image of "walking" suggest? What are these commandments that one must walk in?

5. Reading verses 7-11, the letter takes a more negative turn. In verses 7-8, what is the warning given? What is the deception that they should be concerned about, and what are the consequences?

6. When we turn to verse 9, the Elder encourages abiding in the teachings of Christ and warns against going beyond these teachings. Why might the Elder issue the warning? What does it mean to go beyond? That is, to be a "progressive?" What are the doctrinal/theological issues at stake here?

7. In verses 10 and 11, the Elder deals with a very practical issue, that is hospitality (or the possibility that one should not offer hospitality). What does the Elder call for the community to

do? How do you square this with a text like Hebrews 13:1, which calls for welcoming the stranger?

8.  D. Moody Smith suggests that we might best ignore this advice, as there is enough bigotry and intolerance in our land. On the other hand, Jaime Clark-Soles suggests that at the very least this seeming exclusivist statement might serve to stir a conversation about proper boundaries in congregations. How does a congregation decide what is appropriate and what is inappropriate? Does everything really go, or are there limits?

9.  As the letter closes, what does the Elder write? What do you make of these words? What do they suggest about relationships between congregations? How might we all be part of the same family?

## EXERCISE:

The one distinctive "contribution" of 2 John is this word about refusing hospitality to those who bring false teaching. Using appropriate reference works, such as a bible dictionary, explore the concept of hospitality in the ancient world, and using that information have a conversation about how to appropriately set boundaries in a community of faith. What should be done so that "destructive persons are [not] allowed to wreak havoc on a community with impunity."

## A CALL TO PRAYER:

*May we, having received your love, share that love with our neighbors. We may understand the concern of the letter with welcoming falsehoods into our midst, but even as we seek to be discerning people, may we also show the hospitality that Jesus exhibited in his life.*

## Vision:

3 John is the shortest book of the New Testament. It takes the form of a personal letter, addressing the question of offering hospitality to missionaries, who are dependent on the good will of the Christian communities for support. In this letter, we see two different responses to that call. One is welcome, and the other is exclusion.

## Reading: 3 John

Please read the passage for the day in at least two different translations, a more formal translation, such as the NRSV, CEB, RSV, or NIV, and then read it again in a freer version or paraphrase such as *The Message*, *Phillip's*, or the *New Living Translation*. As you read, pay attention to images that warrant further exploration.

## Lesson:

### Greetings—3 John 1

This third letter attributed by tradition to John is addressed to a particular person. The Elder, whose identity remains shrouded in mystery, writes to the beloved Gaius, commending him for his faithfulness in providing support for traveling missionaries. He also shares his concern about the obstruction offered by Diotrephes to the mission of the church. Finally, we see the Elder commend

Demetrius for his example (as opposed to that of Diotrephes). Jaime Clark-Soles suggests that one could title the letter: "Good Gaius, Dastardly Diotrephes, and Devoted Demetrius."[67]

This is one of only two personal letters in the New Testament, the other being Paul's letter to Philemon. It is also the briefest of the biblical books—only 219 words in the Greek. This is also the only book in the New Testament in which reference is made neither of Jesus or the Christ, making it a rather secular epistle. Although references to "truth" (vs. 1) and "the Name" (vs. 7) could be stand-ins, these are not explicit references. Finally, we should note the belated acceptance of the letter into the New Testament canon.

We do not know much about Gaius, nor the opponent of the Elder, but the letter raises important questions about hospitality and mission and even church governance. While neither Jesus nor Christ are mentioned in the letter, the reference to Truth is surely a substitute, which Gaius and others would understand. Thus, the rendering in the NRSV—whom I love in truth—is probably better than either *The Message* or the *Common English Bible*, which personalizes the love for Gaius: "Whom I truly love."

## Walking in Truth—3 John 2-4

The letter continues with a prayer for Gaius, a common oc-currence in personal letters of that day. The Elder prays that "all may go well with you and that you may be in good health, just as it is well with your soul." The prayer is like others of the day, and isn't specifically Christian. However, the way it is phased and the way it is used has given support to either asceticism or forms of the prosperity gospel.

With this prayer concluded, the Elder writes of his joy at learn-ing from some of the "brothers," (translated in NRSV as friends), that Gaius walks in the Truth. The reference here being to the missionaries whom we will meet later in the letter. Indeed, the

---

67    Jaime Clark-Soles, "1, 2, 3 John" in Gale A. Yee. *Fortress Commentary on the Bible: Two Volume Set* (Kindle Location 57074). Fortress Press. Kindle Edition.

Elder declares that he has "no greater joy than this, to hear that my children are walking in the truth" (vs. 4). In this statement, the Elder declares his full confidence in Gaius and seeks his loyalty as he deals with a problem in the community.

The question that arises here concerns the position of Gaius in the church. There is no reference to ecclesiastical office in the letter, though Gaius, Diotrephes, and Demetrius appear to be leaders of some kind. The differences between Gaius and Diotrephes are seen in the way in which the two receive the Beloved or missionaries into their community. The positions that the two play is unknown and has led to much speculation among scholars. What we can say is that the Elder has full confidence in Gaius' faithfulness and seeks to hold on to his loyalty.

The reference made by the Elder to "walking in truth," refers to living an ethical life. It may also be a reference to having a correct Christology, though there is no evidence here that Diotrephes has an incorrect Christology. Since we do not know the nature of his Christological views, we cannot say for sure whether he was a member of the antichrist party referred to in 1 John and 2 John). Instead, it would appear that the issue here is behavioral. Raymond Brown suggests that regarding the "brothers," Gaius "shows them love and Diotrephes does not."[68] This behavior has been testified to by the "brothers," or "friends," whom we believe from what follows, to have been welcomed by Gaius, despite, perhaps, the opposition of Diotrephes.

## Model of Hospitality—3 John 5-8

With verse five, we come to the heart of the letter. Commendations have been given; now we discover why. The Elder commends Gaius as a model of hospitality for welcoming the brothers and sisters even though they were strangers. This is seen as an act of faithfulness, and it has been reported on by these travelers to the church (*ekklesia*). The Elder wants to encourage Gaius to continue

---

68  Raymond Brown, *Epistles of John (Anchor Bible),* (Garden City, NY: Doubleday and Co., 1982), pp. 705-706.

this hospitality, for to do so is to send them out in a manner worthy of God.

We learn something else about these "friends" who are strangers. They appear to be itinerant missionaries, who are undertaking a "journey for the sake of Christ" (literally: "sake of the Name"). The need for hospitality is found in the decision to accept "no support from unbelievers" (Gentiles). This ministry was intended to be undertaken in such a way that it would not burden unbelievers, but be supported by the churches. That is because, in doing so, "we may become co-workers with the truth." Eugene Peterson translates this verse in a way that makes this even more explicit: "In providing meals and a bed, we become their companions in spreading the Truth" (vs. 8, *The Message*). This word of encouragement to Gaius may be needed because of opposition on the part of some (as we'll see momentarily).

The importance of this word of encouragement is also related to the form that mission took. We know from Paul's letters, it was custom for churches to receive missionaries and provide money and supplies (1 Corinthians 16:6; Romans 15:24). Raymond Brown comments on this form of mission, noting: "While the common-sense attitude would have been to start out with enough money for the whole journey, apparently Christian missionaries were guided by Jesus' own style: 'Jesus ordered them to take nothing for the journey except a staff: no bread, no wallet, no money in their belts' (Mark 6:8)."[69] To help such persons was a form of welcoming Jesus (Matthew 10:40). This raises a question for the contemporary church about the responsibility of support of global mission, supporting those called to preach and teach in faraway places.

## Model of Obstruction of Mission: Diotrephes—3 John 9-12

If Gaius is a model of hospitality who walks in truth (follows in the footsteps of Jesus), then Diotrephes is his opposite. According to the Elder, Diotrephes, "who likes to put himself first, does

---

69   Brown, *Letters of John*, p. 742.

not acknowledge our authority" (vs. 9). It is clear from the text that there is some form of a power struggle between the Elder and Diotrephes. The question raised by the letter concerns the nature of their dispute. From the way that the Elder describes the situation, Diotrephes seems to have usurped power in the congregation. Diotrephes appears to have been spreading rumors about the Elder, thus undermining his authority. He has also been refusing to receive the brothers and sisters who have been sent out by the Elder's church. Thus, the problem with Diotrephes is two-fold. First, he seeks preeminence in the community. Secondly, to attain preeminence in the community he has been spreading rumors and refusing to receive those sent out by the Elder. Not only that, but he is threatening to expel anyone who does receive these emissaries.

The charges that the Elder brings against Diotrephes are interesting considering the instructions given by the Elder in 2 John 10-11, where he instructs the church not to receive those whom he considers heretical. Could it be that Diotrephes has declared the Elder and his supporters to be heretics? As D. Moody Smith points out, "if 2 and 3 John are by the same author, the measures recommended by the Elder in the one letter are being applied to him by Diotrephes in the other."[70] The problem here is that no mention is made of a doctrinal issue. It doesn't seem that they are on the opposite sides theologically, as was the case with the secessionists we meet in the first two letters. That leaves us wondering why this dispute is emerging. Whatever the issue, the letter contrasts the responses of Gaius and Diotrephes. Gaius welcomes the missionaries, but Diotrephes doesn't. This leads to a further question: what is the relationship between these two men? Are they a part of the same congregation? Are they both leaders in the congregation? Has Gaius challenged Diotrephes usurped authority by faithfully welcoming the missionaries, or is he part of another congregation that has been faithful in this way? The letter doesn't help resolve this

---

70  D. Moody Smith, *First, Second, and Third John (Interpretation: A Bible Commentary for Teaching and Preaching)*, (Louisville: John Knox Press, 1991), p. 154.

question. What we do see is that Diotrephes is a negative example when it comes to hospitality. We also learn that the Elder plans to come and settle the matter personally.

This leads us to the third person in the letter—Demetrius. The Elder responds to Diotrephes refusal to welcome the missionaries, as was expected of churches, by offering Gaius a contrasting example of faithful hospitality. The Elder begins the conversation by warning against imitating what is evil: "Beloved, do not imitate what is evil but imitate what is good. Whoever does good is from God; whoever does evil has not seen God" (vs. 11). According to Raymond Brown the Elder "never indicates that Diotrephes is guilty personally of a secessionist distortion of the gospel, but *de facto* Diotrephes' obstructionism is helping the secessionist movement."[71] Of course, Diotrephes might defend himself by suggesting that he is simply trying to be a good shepherd who is protecting the flock against the intrusion of false teachers, in accordance with the instructions we find in 2 John (that would assume that Diotrephes had 2 John in hand). This is the challenge of reading a letter without knowing the full context. We only have the Elder's side of the story, but not that of Diotrephes.

That leads us to Demetrius, who is commended for his faithfulness, which is evidence that the truth (Christ) is in him. So, if Diotrephes is the negative example, Demetrius is the positive one. The Elder wishes to encourage Gaius to follow Demetrius' example and not chose the evil way. It's possible that Demetrius is one of those missionaries Diotrephes has turned away, and thus needing the Elder's recommendation. Raymond Brown writes of this situation:

I have suggested that we may have here the *beginning* of a practice of testimonial letters for Johannine missionaries, so that (in very different ways) both the Presbyter and Diotrephes would be reacting to the need for greater clarity about missionaries, now that secessionist missionaries are also circulating.[72]

---

71  Brown, *Epistles of John,* p. 746.
72  Brown, *Epistles of John,* p. 748.

The concern on the part of the Elder is that even if Diotrephes isn't a secessionist, but resisting people like, perhaps, Demetrius, he is abetting their efforts. Gaius, on the other hand, has demonstrated that he is willing to welcome those sent out on behalf of the church. For that he is commended. All of this leads to the question of proper boundaries. On one hand, there is need to show hospitality and welcome, but there is also the question, which is raised in 2 John, of where to draw the line. Recognizing the need to for wisdom and discernment in showing hospitality to strangers, Joshua Jipp writes that "intentionally placing limitations on our hospitality is a secondary matter that comes *after* we have adequately heard Jesus's call and followed his example as a fried of sinners and outcasts."[73]

## The Promised Visit—3 John 13-14

The letter closes with a promise of a visit. The Elder has more to say on the matters at hand, but they need to be discussed in person rather than by using pen and papers. So, the Elder is planning on a visit (an episcopal visitation?). Having spoken of an impending visit, the Elder closes the letter by sending greetings to Gaius and his friends on behalf of the Elder's congregation. These greetings serve as a reminder of the importance of maintaining community. That Diotrephes is cutting himself off from such community is unfortunate. But, the Elder is hopeful that his engagement with the communities, using his authority, whatever it is, to keep things together so that the work of mission can be extended.

There is much about the letter's context that remains unknown to us. We do not know wrote the letter or the full identity of the recipient. We don't know the date or region out of which the letter emerged. Because the letter was late in gaining entrance to the canon, we cannot say for sure whether it is a first or second century document. Nonetheless, it raises a critical issue, and that has to do with hospitality to strangers and how the church supports those called to teach and preach the gospel. Jaime Clark-Soles makes this

---

73   Joshua W. Jipp, *Saved by Faith and Hospitality*, (Grand Rapids, MI: Wm. B. Eerdmans Publishing Company, 2017), p. 40.

important point regarding the letter and its value for the contemporary church:

Third John addresses questions about hospitality as an ethical imperative for Christians. Christians are called to love not only those whom they know but also those who are "strangers" to them. It also raises questions about how Christians are to support financially those who are called to teach and preach the gospel near and far.[74]

The Elder and Diotrephes, apparently disagree on how these tasks of the church should be addressed. The question remains with us to this day.

## QUESTIONS FOR MEDITATION AND DISCUSSION

1.  As we come to the end of this series of studies, what kind of letter do we find here in 3 John? What do we learn from the first verse that can help us understand who is involved in the conversation?

2.  In verse 2, we have a brief prayer. What are its elements? What message does the prayer suggest? Do you see anything that might be of concern in its message regarding the relationship of health and faith?

3.  The Elder speaks of his joy at reports from some of the "friends" (brothers) about the faithfulness of Gaius. What is the reason for this joy? What does it mean to walk in truth as truth is described in the letter (vs. 3-4)?

4.  From what we read in the first four verses, what do we know about Gaius's role in the church? Does it appear that he has an official role, or is perhaps a layperson?

5.  In verse 5 we come to the heart of the letter. The Elder writes a word of commendation regarding the hospitality shown by

---

74  Jaime Clark-Soles, "1, 2, 3 John," in *Fortress Commentary on the Bible*, (Kindle Locations 57114-57116).

Gaius. What is the nature of this hospitality, and to whom is it shown? What was their response?

6.  In verse 7, we learn something about the recipients of this hospitality. What do we learn first about the purpose of the journey, and secondly the way in which they engaged in this journey? Why might they not accept support from non-believers? When we compare this account with the account of the sending out of the twelve in Mark 6:6b-13, what do you notice? Do you see similarities?

7.  If the missionaries do not seek support from the nonbelievers (perhaps the ones they seek to evangelize), how should the churches respond? (vs. 8). How does the reading from *The Message* clarify this?

8.  Do you see anything in verses 5-8 that speak to the contemporary church about support for those who engage in preaching and teaching faraway places? What responsibility do churches have for supporting missions?

9.  If Gaius is a positive example of hospitality, what do you make of Diotrephes? Why does the Elder condemn him? Is it fair? What do we learn about him?

10. Do you see here any signs of a power struggle between Diotrephes and the Elder? What is the nature of this struggle? Do you think this is fair?

11. In 2 John 10-11, the Elder tells the Elect Lady not to receive anyone who doesn't bring the same teaching (Christology) as he brings into their homes. How is Diotrephes different or the same?

12. As the letter nears its closing, the Elder returns to the commendation of Gaius by telling him not to imitate evil, but good, for these signal one's relationship with God. Does this seem familiar? Is it similar to the words in 1 John about love?

13. Finally, we hear about Demetrius. What does the Elder say about Demetrius? What role does he play in the story? Raymond Brown suggests this word about Demetrius is a sign that letters of recommendation might be emerging, and that the reference here is to support Demetrius. Why might letters of reference be needed? Do both the Elder and Diotrephes have reason to be leery about strangers knocking the door?

14. In verses 13-15 we read the Elder's closing. What does the Elder write, and what do you take from these words? What message emerges?

15. Having walked through the Johannine letters, what themes have emerged? What is your takeaway from this journey with the one we call John?

## EXERCISE:

The letter speaks about hospitality given to missionaries, people are often strangers to a local congregation. Find the website of either a denominational missions organization or another similar organization. Using this source find out what the missionaries do, what training is required, and discover how they are supported. Then compare this with what we read here. What differences do you notice? What word of wisdom do you take from the letter that speaks to our contemporary mission work?

## A CALL TO PRAYER:

*May we, like Gaius, be known for our hospitality. Instill in us that quality of life that is rooted in love.*

ALSO FROM ENERGION PUBLICATIONS
by Robert D. Cornwall

The Triune
Nature of
God

CONVERSATIONS REGARDING THE TRINITY
BY A DISCIPLES OF CHRIST PASTOR/THEOLOGIAN

Robert D. Cornwall

Topical
Line
Drives

Volume 37

This short volume is valuable to all those who seek to understand the trinity not just as an element in a doctrinal system, but as it aids us in thinking about elements of our faith.

Bob Cornwall provides a vision for today's Christians, centered around living out our gifts in creative and life-transforming ways. We are gifted, even when we are unaware of it.
Bruce Epperly, PhD
Pastor and Author

Unfettered Spirit
Spiritual Gifts for the New Great Awakening

ROBERT D. CORNWALL

FOREWORD BY BRUCE G. EPPERLY

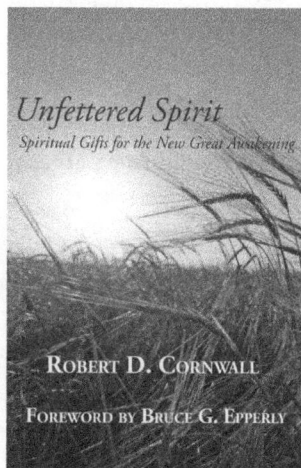

# MORE FROM ENERGION PUBLICATIONS

**ACADEMY OF PARISH CLERGY SERIES AND AUTHORS**

### Conversations in Ministry
| | | |
|---|---|---|
| Clergy Table Talk | Kent Ira Groff | $9.99 |
| Out of the Office | Robert D. Cornwall | $9.99 |
| Wind and Whirlwind | David Moffett-Moore | $9.99 |

### Guides to Practical Ministry
| | | |
|---|---|---|
| Overcoming Sermon Block | William Powell Tuck | $12.99 |
| Thrive | Ruth Fletcher | $14.99 |
| In Changing Times | Ron Higdon | $14.99 |

### Academy Member Authors (Selected Titles)
| | | |
|---|---|---|
| Faith in the Public Square | Robert D. Cornwall | $16.99 |
| Ephesians: A Participatory Study Guide | | $9.99 |
| Ultimate Allegiance | | $9.99 |
| The Authority of Scripture in a Postmodern Age | | $5.99 |
| From Words of Woe to Unbelievable News | | $5.99 |
| The Eucharist | | $5.99 |
| Unfettered Spirit | | $14.99 |
| From Here to Eternity | Bruce Epperly | $5.99 |
| Angels, Mysteries, and Miracles | | $9.99 |
| Transforming Acts | | $14.99 |
| Jonah: When God Changes | | $5.99 |
| Process Theology: Embracing Adventure with God | | $5.99 |
| The Journey to the Undiscovered Country | William Powell Tuck | $9.99 |
| Lord, I Keep Getting a Busy Signal | | $9.99 |
| The Last Words from the Cross | | $9.99 |
| The Church Under the Cross | | $9.99 |
| Creation in Contemporary Experience | David Moffett-Moore | $9.99 |
| Life as Pilgrimage | | $14.99 |
| The Spirit's Fruit | | $9.99 |
| The Jesus Manifesto | | $9.99 |
| Spiritual Care Reflections | Charles J. Lopez, Jr. | $14.99 |
| Surviving a Son's Suicide | Ron Higdon | $9.99 |
| All I Need to Know I'm Still Learning at 80 | | |

Generous Quantity Discounts Available
Dealer Inquiries Welcome
Energion Publications — P.O. Box 841
Gonzalez, FL_ 32560
Website: http://energionpubs.com
Phone: (850) 525-3916

www.ingramcontent.com/pod-product-compliance
Lightning Source LLC
LaVergne TN
LVHW011204080426
835508LV00007B/599

* 9 7 8 1 6 3 1 9 9 6 8 8 7 *